The
20th Anniversary Edition
offers:

Fresh Designs
Pattern Variations
Numerous Templates
Size Options

Bargello Variation

Chained Melody

Jazzy Jolt

Cheryl Phillips
Phillips Fiber Art Publishing

www.phillipsfiberart.com

ISBN 988673809-X
9 780988 673809 90000

Thread

For piecing, choose a thread type to match your fabric. A finer piecing thread, such as two ply 60 weight 100% cotton or fine polyester is suggested.

Batting

Use one-hundred percent cotton batting for smoother, flatter wall hangings and quilts.

Notions and Equipment

- A sewing machine with balanced tension
- ¼" presser foot
- An iron and ironing board
- A Ten Degree Wedge tool
- A clear acrylic ruler (6" x 24")
- A rotary cutter (45mm, 18mm)
- A cutting mat (at least 18" x 24")
- Non-slip adhesive product or wide transparent packaging tape
- Freezer paper
- Fusible interfacing
- Permanent gel pen or felt tip pen for marking on the wedge ruler
- Mechanical pencil with fine, soft lead

Wedge Tool

Instructions in the ***20th Anniversary Quilts Without Corners Platinum Edition*** are written for the Ten Degree Wedge tool. The Ten Degree Wedge tool can be found in most quilt and fabric shops. The tool is also available directly from Phillips Fiber Art.

Printed Templates

Printed templates for the mini Ten Degree Wedge, wedge extension, framing template, and mini thirty degree wedge for making pieced quilt centers are found on page 56. Acrylic tools for these templates are also available directly from Phillips Fiber Art.

Overview

What follows is a brief overview of how to make the quilts in this book. More detailed instructions, basic to all the patterns, are found at the back of the book.

Step One

Sewing the Strip Sets

You will measure, cut and label strips of fabric. The word *width* in the Cutting Section refers to the width of the fabric, selvage to selvage, (about 40" to 44") depending on manufacturer. Then you'll sew sets of these strips together with an exact ¼" seam allowance.

Step Two

Cutting the Wedges

This requires precision. Before cutting, you'll want to put non-slip adhesive product or wide loops of transparent tape on the back of the wedge tool so it won't slip around on your fabric. Then you'll cut out identical wedges by placing the ruler on the fabric as shown in the pattern illustrations.

Step Three

Constructing the Circle

You will see the design develop as you sew the wedges together. Again, ***exact*** ¼" seams will prevent a problem later on. Carefully sew the 36 wedges together to form a circle. Press the circle from the back with all seams going in one direction, being careful not to distort the symmetry. Appliqué a center to form a beautiful circular quilt top.

Step Four

Finishing

You'll layer the top, batting and back, and quilt by machine or hand and bind the edge.

Enjoy!

Bargello
Creative Option
using six color families
(first quilt)
Page 14

Bargello
Creative Option
using six color families
(second quilt)
Page 14

Bargello
Creative Option
using solid color wedges
with six color families
Page 15

Bargello
Creative Option
using solid color wedges
with six color families
Page 15

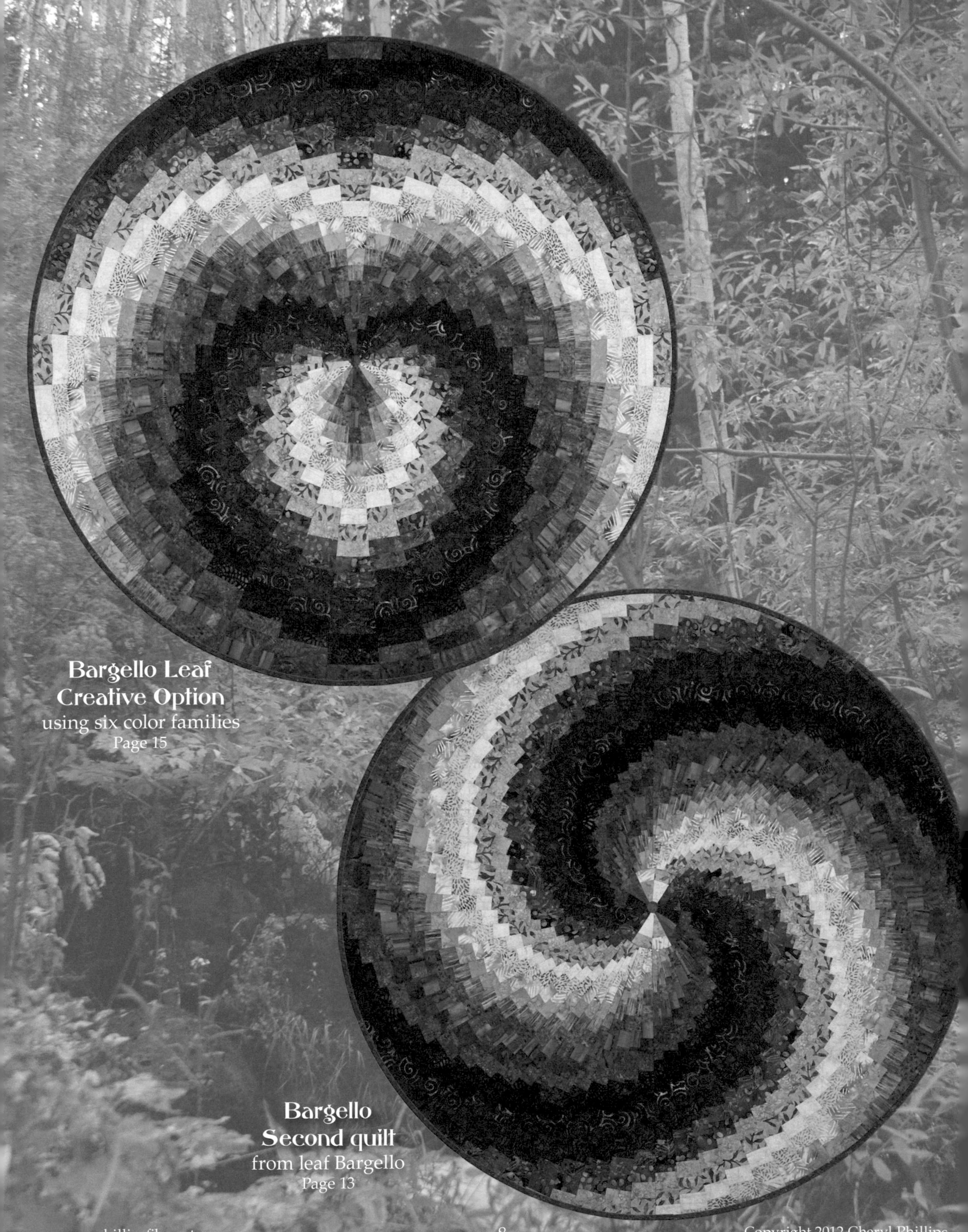

Bargello Leaf Creative Option
using six color families
Page 15

Bargello Second quilt
from leaf Bargello
Page 13

Bargello in the Round

Be sure to read over both the introduction, pages 4 and 5 and the basic instructions, pages 54 to 57 before beginning your project.

Finished Circles
First: 50″ in diameter
Second: 48″ in diameter

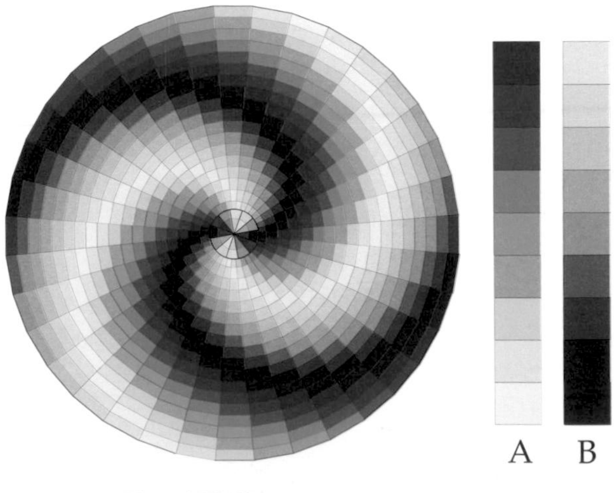

Fabric

Color Family A
Nine pieces .... 1/2 yd each [11" actual]

Color Family B
Nine pieces .... 1/2 yd each [11" actual]

Binding.. 1/2 yd for each quilt
Backing.. 3 yd for each quilt
Batting .... 54" x 54" for each quilt

Fabric Selection

Select nine values of two complimentary color families. Arrange each color family group by value, grading from very light to very dark.

Cutting

- Cut ***six*** strips of each fabric across the width of the fabric.
- Cut strips from several layered fabrics at a time as all strips are cut the same width.

Color Family A

Six strips of each fabric .... 1 3/4" wide

Color Family B

Six strips of each fabric ....1 3/4" wide

- Arrange Color Family A from dark to light, followed by Color Family B from light to dark.

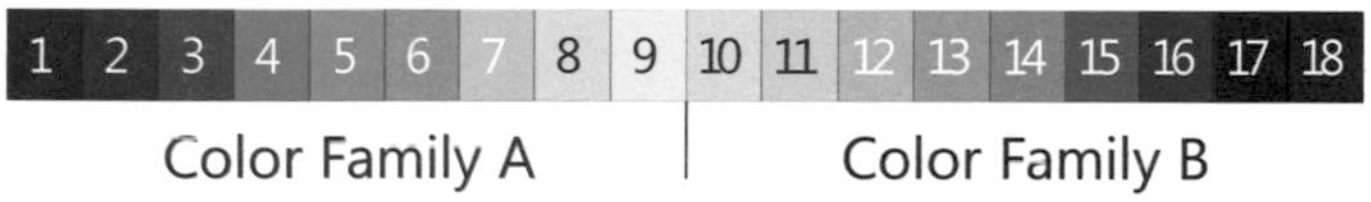

Step One Sewing the Strip Sets

Sew **exact** ¼" seams throughout.

Sections 1-18

1. Sew ***six*** strip sets in the order shown.
2. Press the seam allowances in one direction.
3. **Sparingly** straighten the sides of each strip set. The strip set must measure at least 39".
4. Cut ***six*** 6 ½" sections from each strip set.

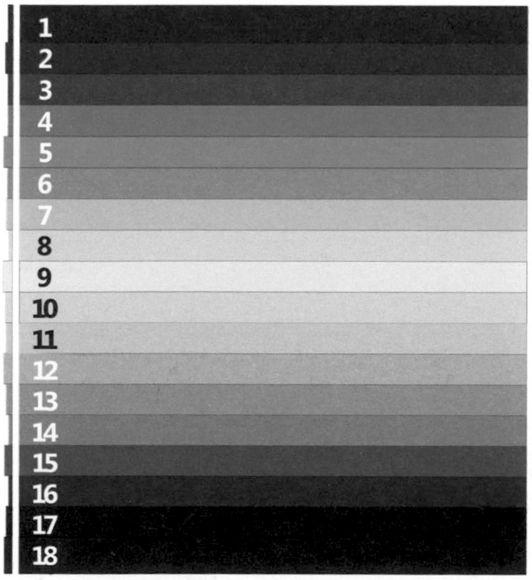

Trim sparingly

Cut six per strip set

Keep it organized!

Organization is the key to this project.
Tape snippets of fabric to an index card and number.
Separate sections in two stacks.

Making Tubes

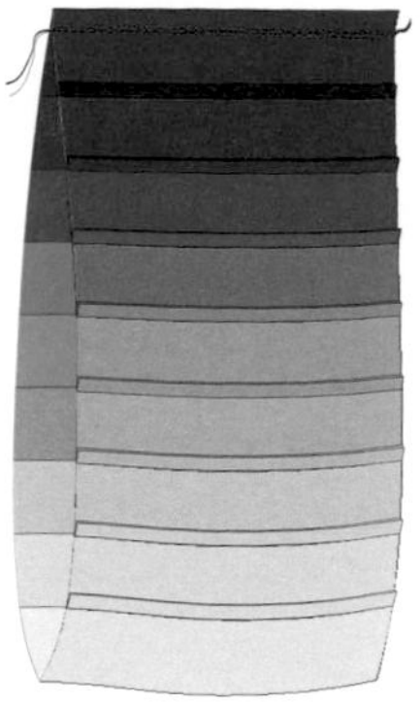

1. Set aside two of the 6 ½" pieces for ***two*** #1 Sections.
2. Label each as #1.
3. Sew the other sections into tubes. The darkest fabric from Color Family A will be sewn to the darkest fabric from Color Family B.

Opening Sections

1. Open each tube at the joining seam as listed.

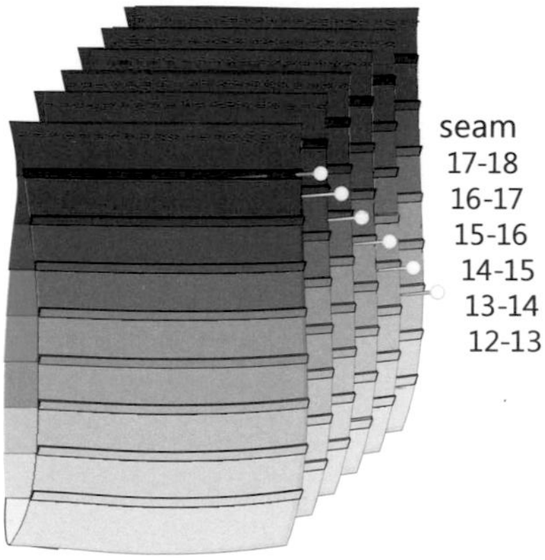

Mark each seam to be removed with a pin.

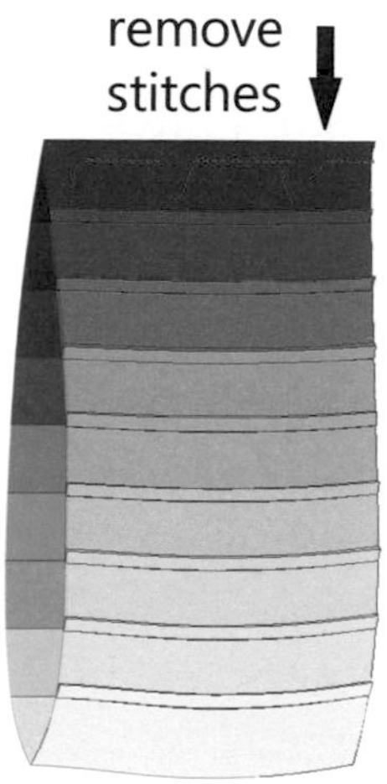

Open two #2	Sections at seam 17-18	Label as 2
Open two #3	Sections at seam 16-17	Label as 3
Open two #4	Sections at seam 15-16	Label as 4
Open two #5	Sections at seam 14-15	Label as 5
Open two #6	Sections at seam 13-14	Label as 6
Open two #7	Sections at seam 12-13	Label as 7
Open two #8	Sections at seam 11-12	Label as 8
Open two #9	Sections at seam 10-11	Label as 9
Open two #10	Sections at seam 9-10............	Label as 10
Open two #11	Sections at seam 8-9.............	Label as 11
Open two #12	Sections at seam 7-8.............	Label as 12
Open two #13	Sections at seam 6-7.............	Label as 13
Open two #14	Sections at seam 5-6.............	Label as 14
Open two #15	Sections at seam 4-5.............	Label as 15
Open two #15	Sections at seam 3-4.............	Label as 16
Open two #17	Sections at seam 2-3	Label as 17
Open two #18	Sections at seam 1-2	Label as 18

Each section begins with a new fabric to create the bargello effect.

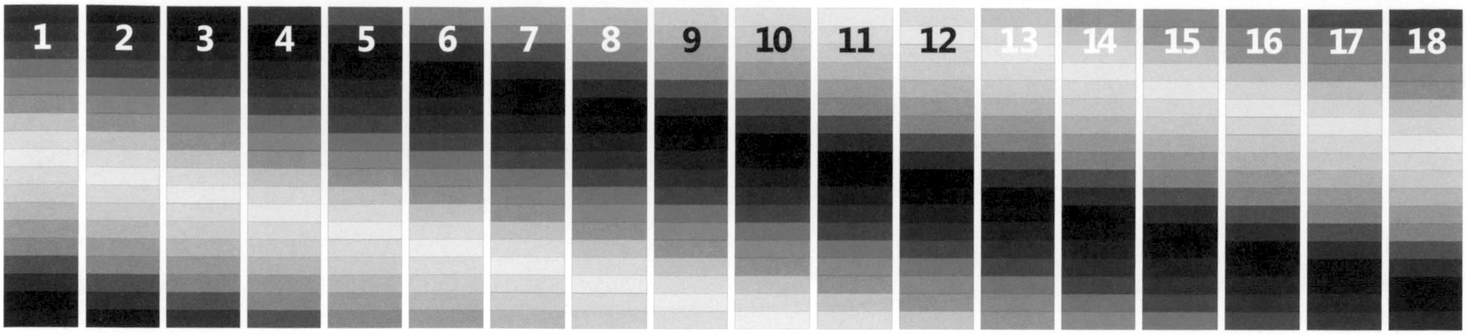

2. Label each section by number on the ***top*** of the section to avoid turning it upside down.
3. Press the seam allowances in the opposite direction for the ***even*** numbered sections.

Keep it organized!

Download labels for this project from our web site. See inside of back cover.

Group the wedges below in four stacks: two groups of wedges and two groups of scrap pieces.

Step Two Cutting Wedges

1. Center the wedge tool to the strip with seam lines parallel to the tool markings.
2. Cut a fabric wedge and label with the section number.
3. Repeat the steps for the remaining 6 ½" strips.

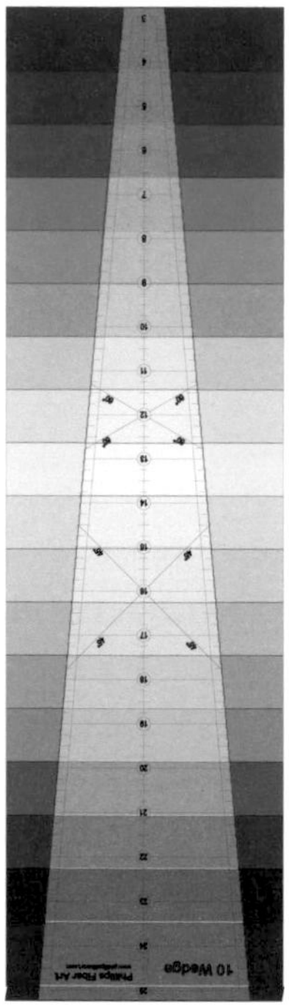

Center the wedge tool

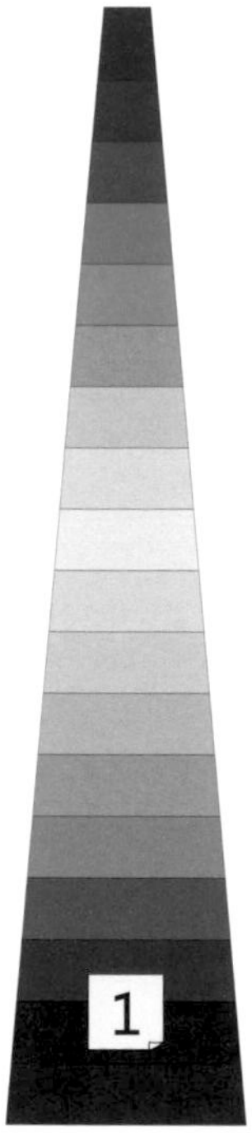

fabric wedge

4. Set aside the scrap pieces for a second quilt.
5. Pin the sets together and label.

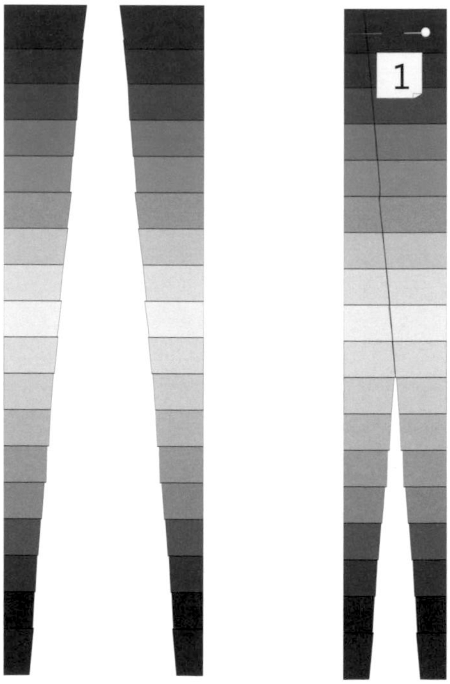

save scraps for second circle

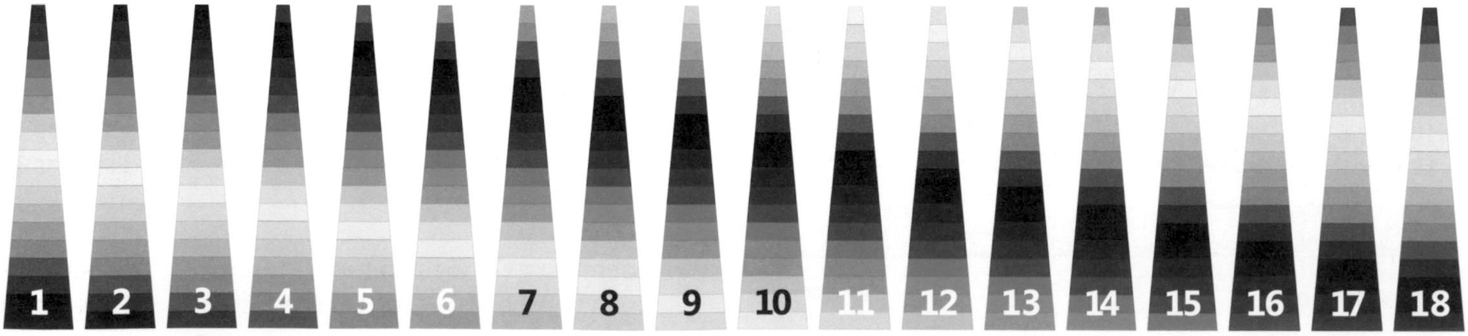

Step Three Constructing the Circle

1. Place wedge #2 onto wedge #1.
2. Pin as needed, matching seams.
3. Sew the wedges together.
4. Continue sewing the wedges in order shown until your circle is complete.
5. After the top is complete, press from the back with seam allowances going in a counterclockwise direction. Press again from the front.

Find tips on Pressing on page 55.

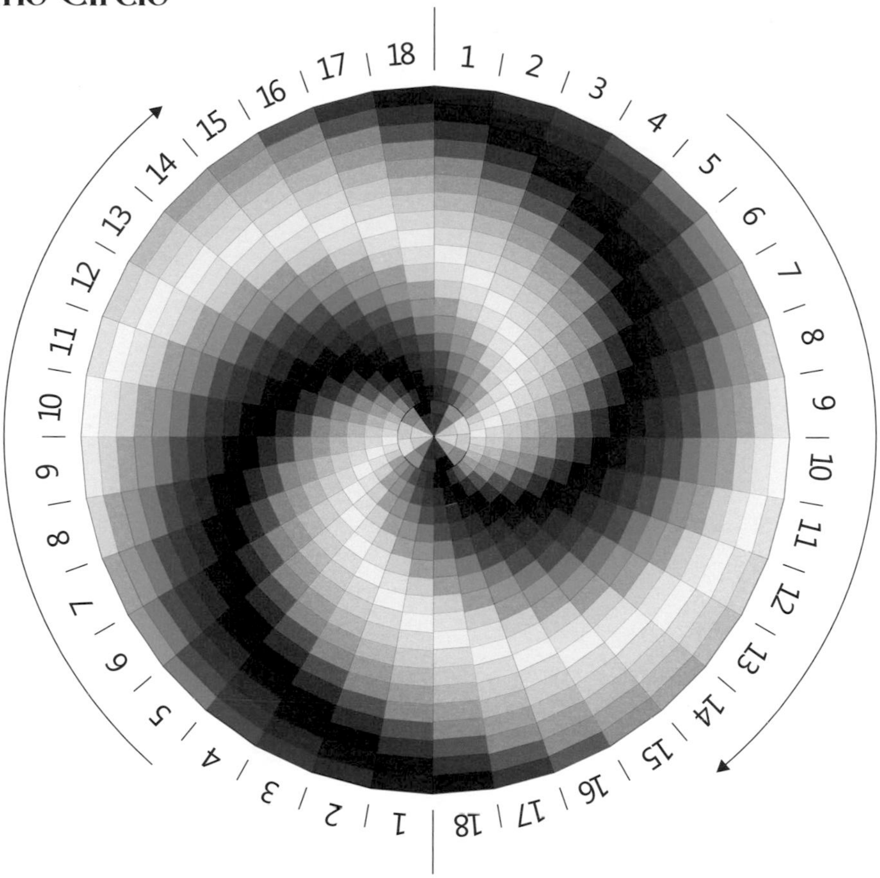

The Center Applique

1. Cut one 2 ½" x 6" piece from each fabric:
   1, 4, 7, 10, 13, and 16.
2. Cut one 1 ¾" x 6" piece from each fabric:
   2, 5, 8, 11, 14, and 17.
3. Make ***six*** small strip sets as shown.
4. Trace the Mini 30 Degree Wedge found on page 61 onto template plastic.
5. Cut ***two*** wedge shapes per strip set.
6. Sew the wedges to make a circle.
7. Refer to the *Piecing Center Appliqué* instructions found on page 56.

You may substitute a coordinating motif or one of the main fabrics as your center applique.

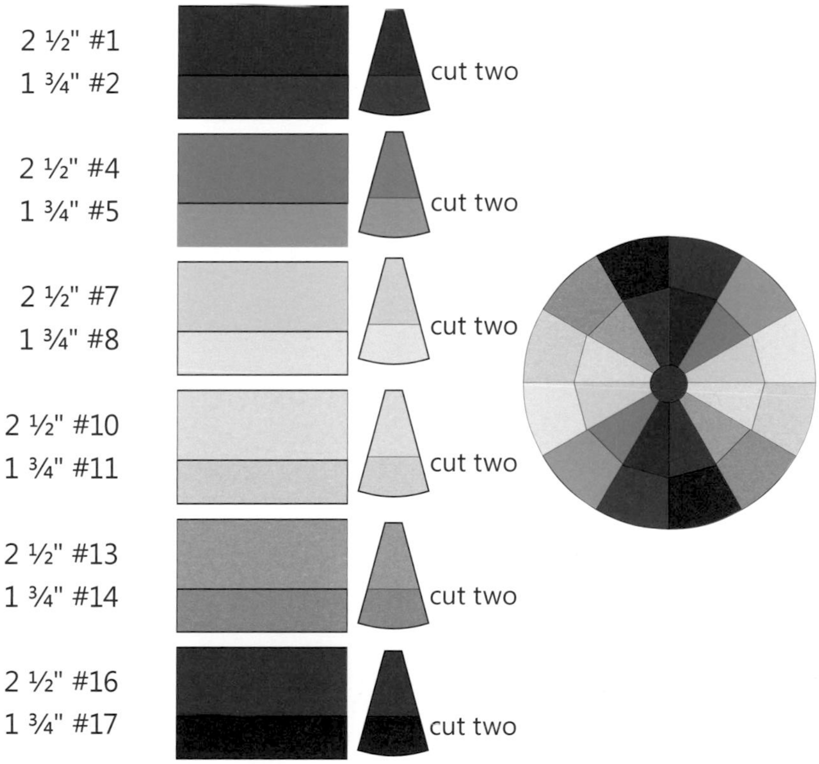

Step Four Finishing

The Bargello quilt top is now ready for the finishing process. You will find the help you need in the *Basic Instructions* on page 56.

Making the Second Circle

Step One Sewing Leftover Pieces

Use the leftover pieces from the first Bargello circle to make an interesting second quilt.

1. Place the leftover pair together, aligning the straight sides. Offset the upper wedge with the seams aligned to the center of the strips below.
2. With right sides together, sew the pair together along the straight sides.

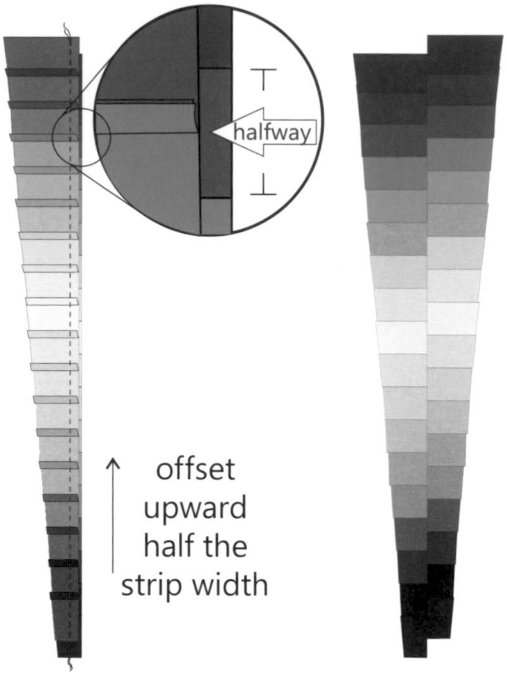

Step Two Cutting Wedges

1. Center the wedge tool to the new section, with the wide end of the tool extending beyond the fabric as necessary. Note the offset section is shorter than the wedge tool.
2. Cut the fabric wedge. Trim the wide end to make the top straight.
3. Label each new wedge.

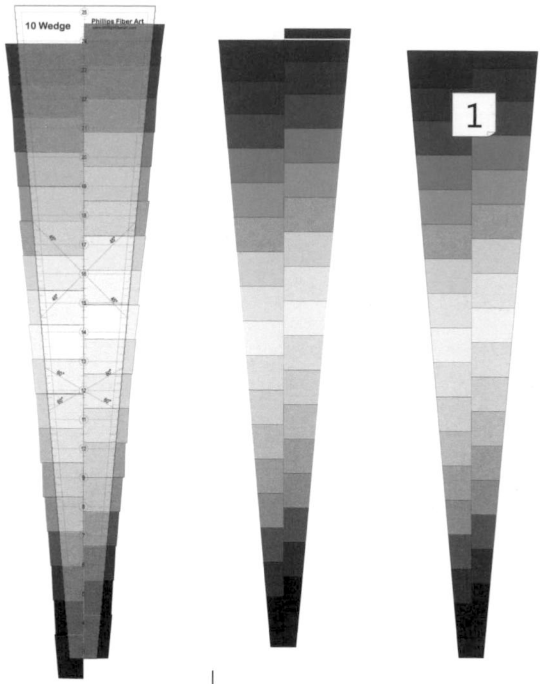

Step Three Constructing the Circle

1. Sew the wedges together in the order shown.
2. Make a center appliqué following the instructions on the previous page.

Note: *The second quilt will be slightly smaller than the first.*

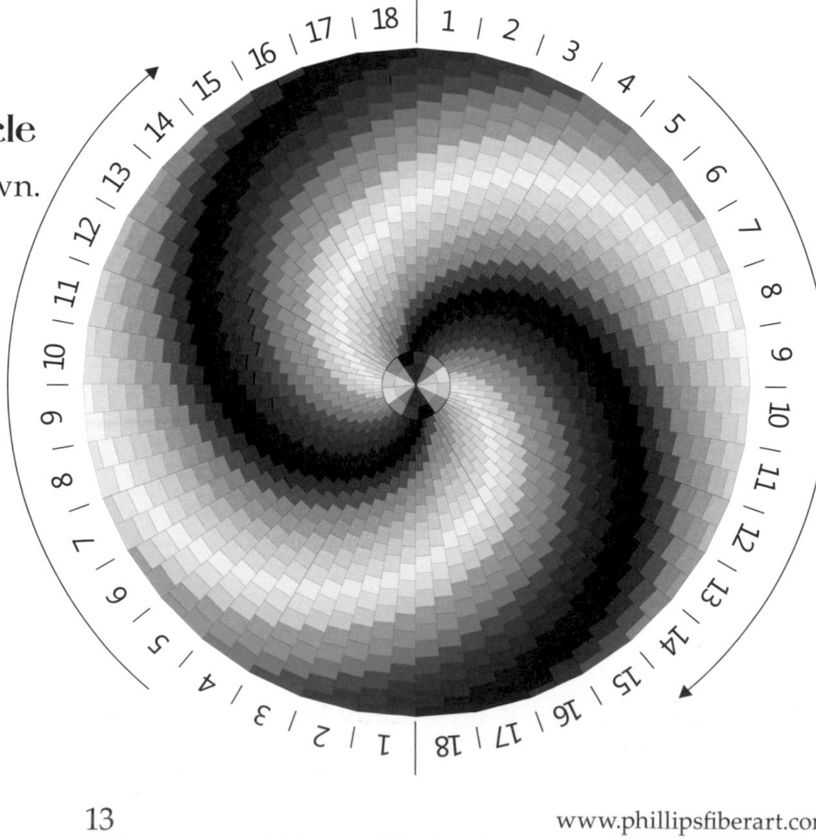

Creative Option

Making only the "Second Circle"

To make just one circle with the complexity of the second version, follow these suggestions:

Make 6 ½" sections as shown on page 10. Cut in half vertically to make two 3 ¼" sections. Use these in place of the leftover pieces from above. Continue with the steps found on this page to make the circle.

Creative Options

The next four pages are intended only to inspire the creative quilter who wants to expand limits and try more than recipe quilt designs.

Changing the Quilt Size

24" Bargello in the Round

To make one 24" Bargello circle, use the Ten Degree Mini Wedge tool or the 12" line on your regular wedge tool.

Suggested yardage for the 18 fabrics is ¼ yard each.

Cut the strips as listed but reduce the size to 1" wide.

Sew ***three*** strip sets, then cross cut the strip sets into 3" wide pieces.

Follow Steps Two and Three as stated in the basic pattern.

59" Bargello in the Round

To make one 59" Bargello circle, use the Ten Degree Wedge tool with the Ten Degree Wedge Extension attached. See page 63 for the extension template.

Suggested yardage for the 18 fabrics is ⅝ yard each.

Cut the strips as listed but increase the size to 2" wide.

Sew ***six*** strip sets, then cross cut the strip sets into 6 ½" wide pieces.

Cut wedges following the 29 ½" line.

Follow the remaining portions of Steps Two and Step Three as stated in the basic pattern.

68" Bargello in the Round

To make one 68" Bargello circle, use the Ten Degree Wedge tool with the Ten Degree Wedge Extension attached. See page 63 for the extension template.

Suggested yardage for the 18 fabrics is ¾ yard each.

Cut the strips as listed but increase the size to 2 ¼" wide.

Sew ***eight*** strip sets, then cross cut the strip sets into 7 ¼" wide pieces.

Cut wedges following the 34" line.

Follow the remaining portions of Steps Two and Step Three as stated in the basic pattern.

Color Variations

Color variations offer the simplest creative options for the Bargello design. Here are a few favorites.

Three Color Families

Rather than two main color families, this variation uses three groups of six fabrics. Each group grades from light to dark fabrics within its color family. The yardage and cutting requirements remain the same.

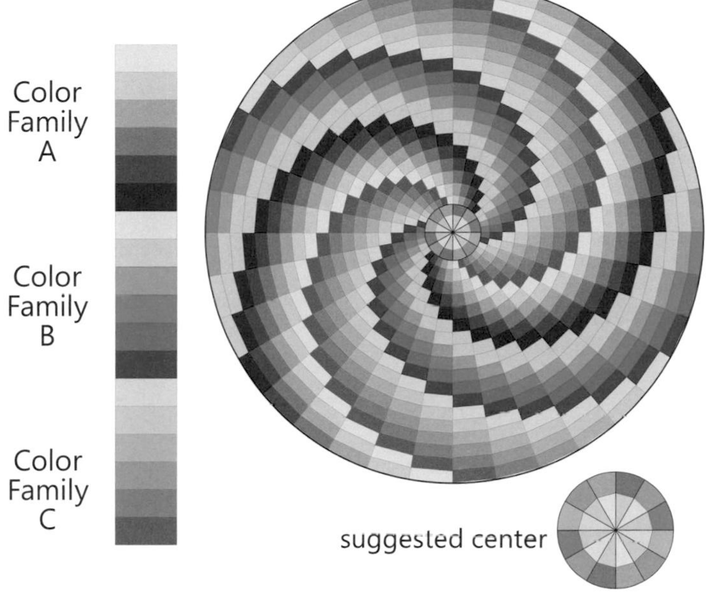

Six Color Families

Rather than using two main color families, this variation uses six groups of three fabrics. Each group uses a light, medium, and dark value of each color. The yardage and cutting requirements remain the same.

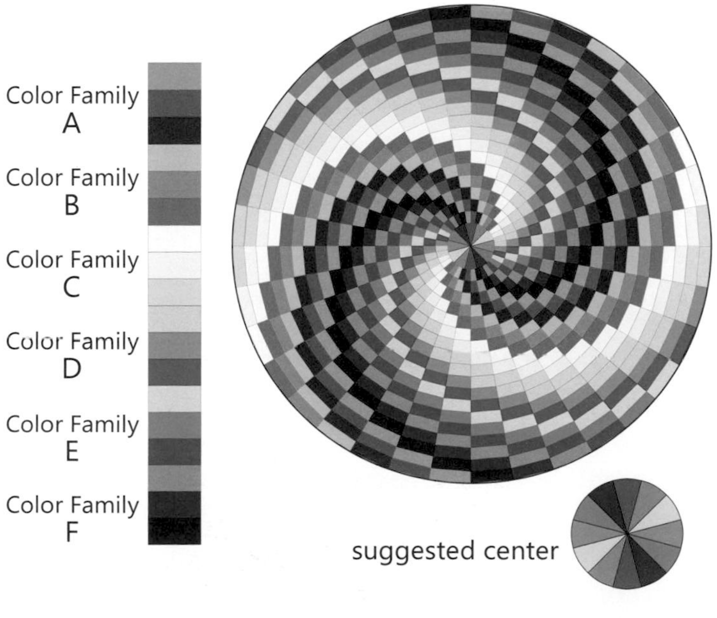

Rearranging the Wedges

Simply rearrange the wedges to get the illusion of a leaf or heart. Make the wedges as stated in the basic instructions, but assemble them in the order shown. Note the placement of wedges 17 and 18.

Two Color Families

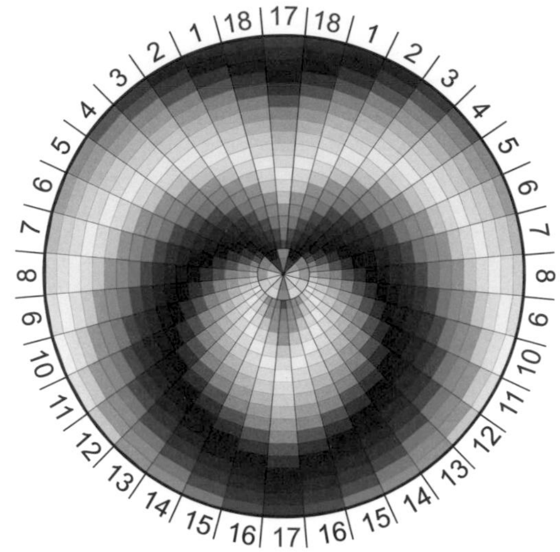

Three Color Families

Six Color Families

Adding Solid Wedges

Save time and fabric! No seams to match!

Select any variation: two, three or six color families. Cut and sew half the number of the strips and strip sets suggested. Combine 18 pieced wedges and 18 solid wedges. The solid wedge fabric requires 1 3/8 yards if non-directional or 2 yards for one way design fabric.

Two Color Families

Three Color Families

Six Color Families

Windmill Swirl

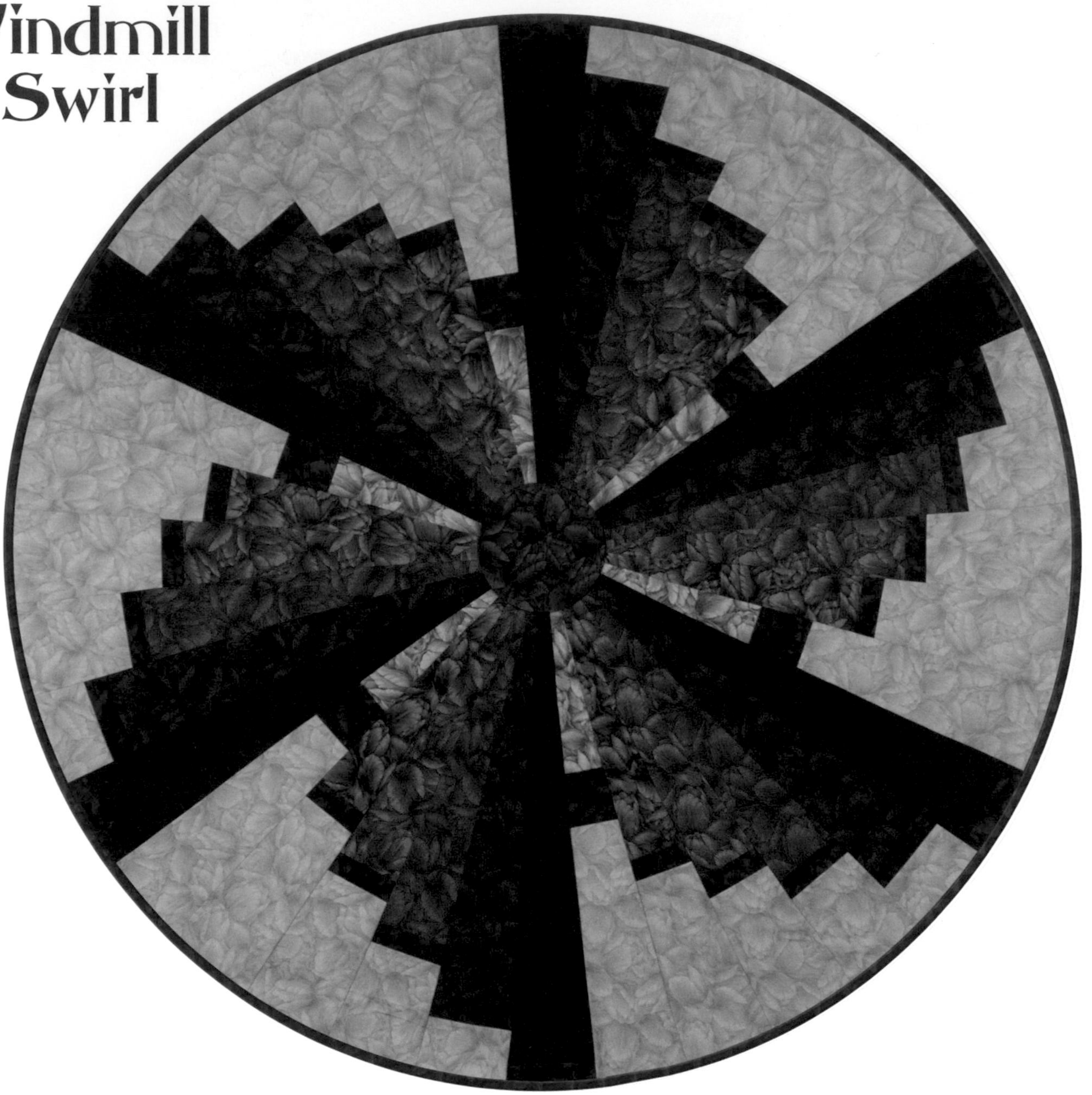

Be sure to read over both the introduction, pages 4 and 5, and the basic instructions, pages 54 to 57 before beginning your project.

Finished Circle
50" in diameter

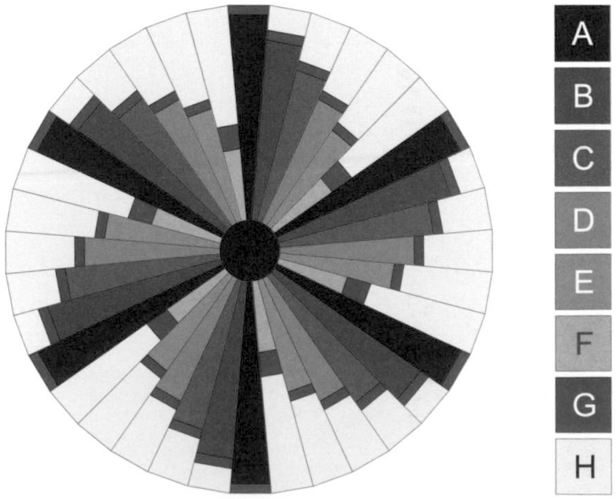

Fabric

Color A	3/4 yd	[22" actual]
Color B	2/3 yd	[19" actual]
Color C	5/8 yd	[17" actual]
Color D	1/2 yd	[15" actual]
Color E	1/2 yd	[13" actual]
Color F	1/3 yd	[8" actual]
Color G	3/8 yd	[11" actual]
Color H	1 1/4 yd	[38" actual]
Binding	1/2 yd	
Backing	3 yd	
Batting	54" sq	

Cutting

Cut Strips in the widths as shown below. Group and label the strips according to width and color.

Color A

One Strip....................................21 1/2" x width

Color B

One Strip..19" x width

Color C

One Strip....................................16 1/2" x width

Color D

One Strip....................................14 1/2" x width

Color E

One Strip....................................12 1/2" x width

Color F

One Strip.. 8" x width

Color G

One strip .... 3" x width
Five strips....................................1 1/2" x width

Color H

One Strip....................................12 1/2" x width
One Strip......................................9 1/2" x width
One Strip......................................7 1/2" x width
One Strip......................................5 1/2" x width
One Strip.. 3" x width

Step One Sewing the Strip Sets

- Sew ***exact*** ¼" seams through out.
- Label all strip sets as shown.

Strip Sets 1-6

1. Sew Strip Set 1 in the order shown.
   Press the seam allowances toward the G fabric.
2. Sew Strip Sets 2-6 as shown.
   Press the seam allowances toward the H fabric.

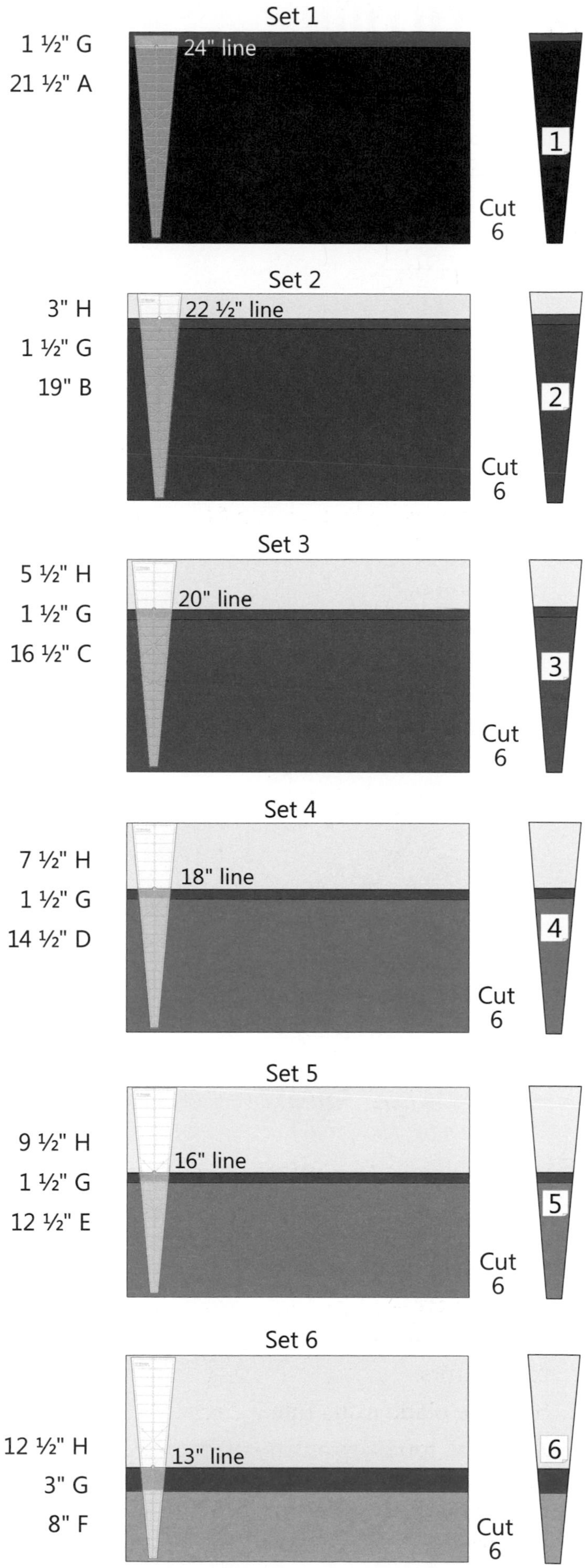

Step Two   Cutting the Wedges

Prepare the wedge tool as suggested on page 54.

Strip Sets 1-6

1. Place the 24" line of the wedge tool on G/A seam of Strip Set 1.
   Cut ***six*** wedges. Label as #1.
2. Place the 22 ½" line of the wedge tool on H/G seam of Strip Set 2.
   Cut ***six*** wedges. Label as #2.
3. Place the 20" line of the wedge tool on H/G seam of Strip Set 3.
   Cut ***six*** wedges. Label as #3.
4. Place the 18" line of the wedge tool on H/G seam of Strip Set 4.
   Cut ***six*** wedges. Label as #4.
5. Place the 16" line of the wedge tool on H/G seam of Strip Set 5.
   Cut ***six*** wedges. Label as #5.
6. Place the 13" line of the wedge tool on H/G seam of Strip Set 6.
   Cut ***six*** wedges. Label as #6.

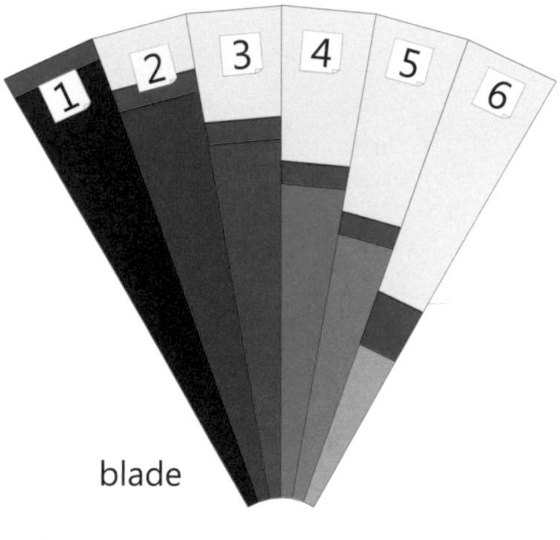

Step Three   Constructing the Circle

Sewing Wedges

1. Lay out ***six*** wedges in order.
2. Sew the ***six*** wedges together to form a blade.
3. Repeat for the remaining wedges for ***six*** blade units.
4. Sew the blade units into a circle.
5. After the top is complete, press from the back with seam allowances going in a counterclockwise direction. Press again from the front.

Find tips on Pressing on page 55.

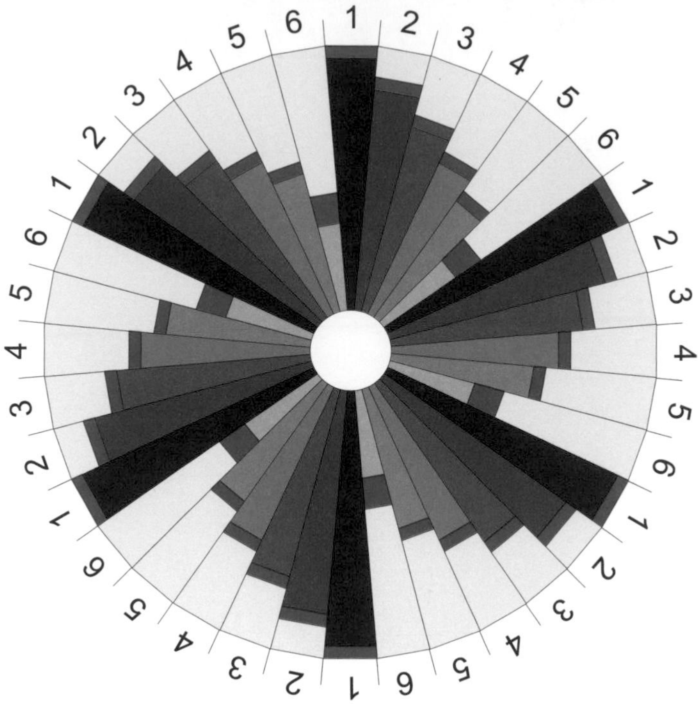

Center Applique

- Trace the circle from page 61 for your center applique.
- Make the applique with leftover Fabric A.
- Applique the circle to the center of the quilt.

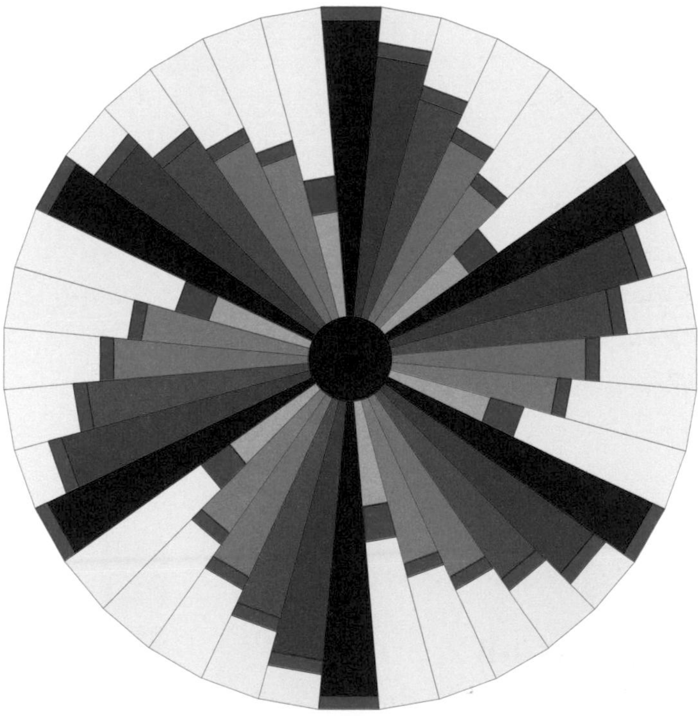

Step Four   Finishing

The Windmill quilt top is now ready for the finishing process. You will find the help you need in the *Basic Instructions* on page 56.

Speedy Spiral Tree Skirt

Be sure to read over both the introduction, pages 4 and 5 and the basic instructions, pages 54 to 57 before beginning your project.

Finished Circle
42″ in diameter

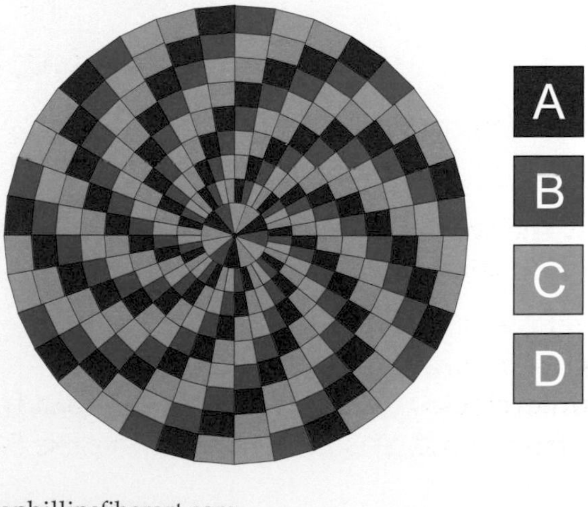

Fabric

Color A	7/8 yd	[25" actual]
Color B	7/8 yd	[25" actual]
Color C	7/8 yd	[25" actual]
Color D	7/8 yd	[25" actual]
Binding (for center and opening)*	1/2 yd	
Backing	1 5/8 yd	
Batting	46" x 46"	

**Sample trimmed with folded edging made with remaining fabric*

Cutting

Cut Strips in the widths as shown below. Group and label the strips according to width and color.

Color A

One Strip*.. 2 1/2" x width
Eight Strips...................................... 2 3/4" x width

Color B

One Strip*.. 2 1/2" x width
Eight Strips .... 2 3/4" x width

Color C

One Strip*.. 2 1/2" x width
Eight Strips .... 2 3/4" x width

Color D

One Strip*.. 2 1/2" x width
Eight Strips...................................... 2 3/4" x width

** used for the Folded Edging found on page 22*

Step One   Sewing the Strip Sets

- Sew ***exact*** ¼" seams through out.
- Label each strip set by number on the ***top*** of each set to avoid turning it upside down.

Strip Sets 1-4

1. Sew each strip set in order.
2. Make sure the strip order in each strip set agrees with the illustrations before ironing and cutting.
3. Press Strip Sets 1 and 3 toward the top.
4. Press Strip Sets 2 and 4 toward the bottom.
5. Label each strip set, noting the top of the strip set.

Step Two   Cutting the Wedges

1. Place your wedge tool on Strip Set 1 as shown. Note the wide end of the wedge extends beyond the strip set.
2. Cut ***nine*** identical wedges.
3. Group and label as 1.
4. Repeat for Strip Sets 2, 3, and 4 as shown.

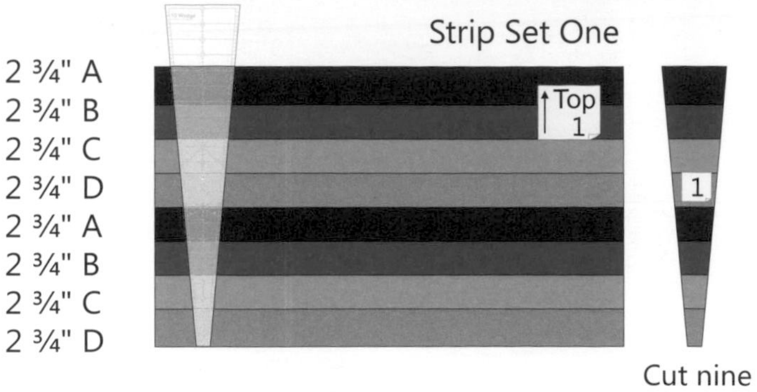

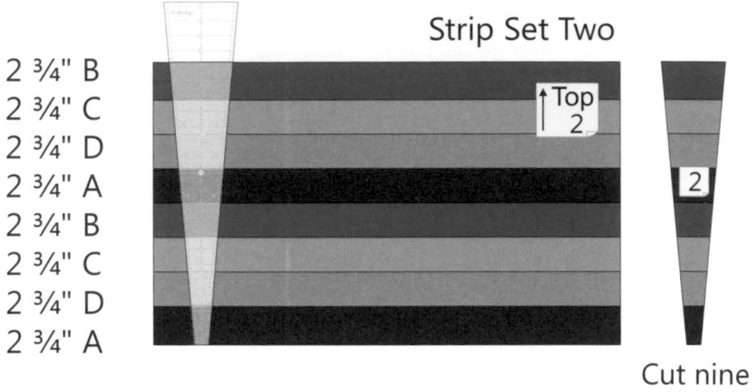

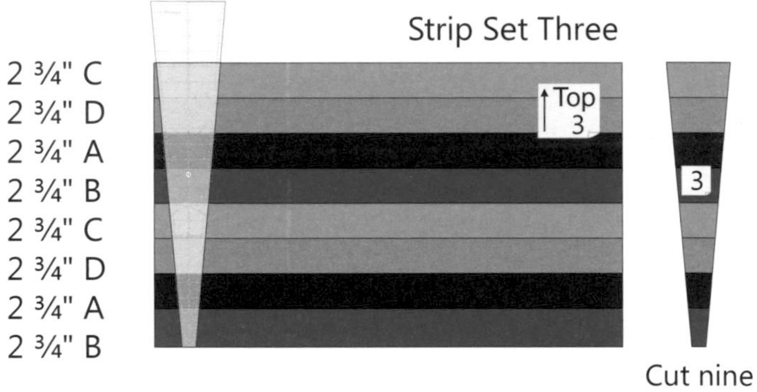

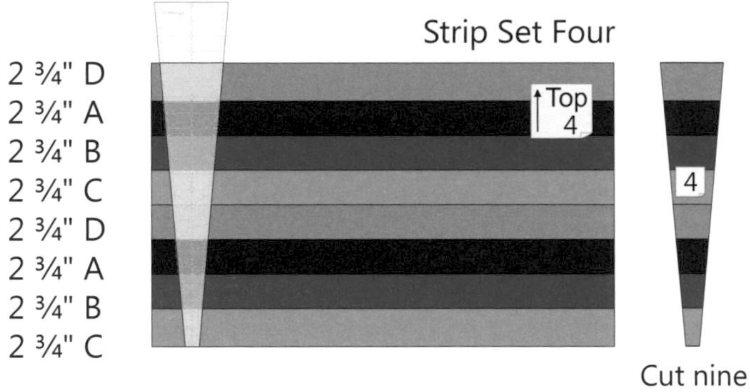

Step Three   Constructing the Circle

Sewing Wedges

1. Lay out the wedges in order.
2. Sew the wedges together, leaving one side open to slip around your tree.
3. After the top is complete, press from the back with seam allowances going in a counterclockwise direction. Press again from the front. Find tips on ***Pressing*** on page 54.

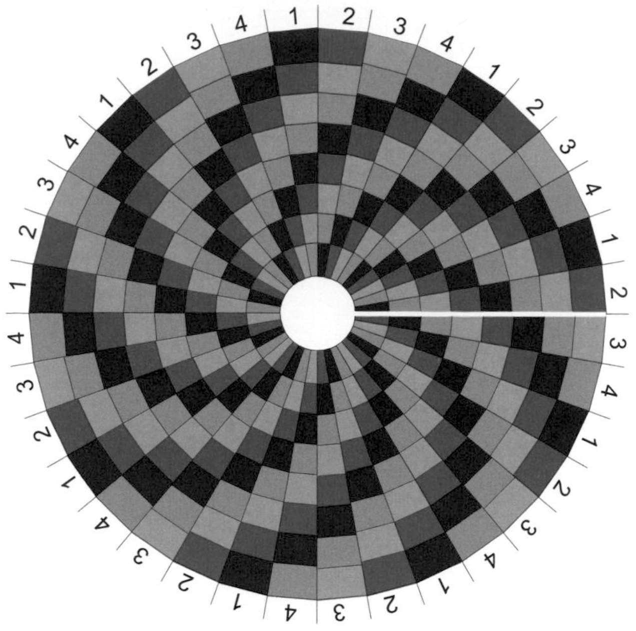

Step Four Finishing

Binding

- Cut 2 ½" wide bias strips from the binding fabric. Sew strips together for a length of at least 60 inches. Bind the inside circle and the two open sides.

Folded Edging

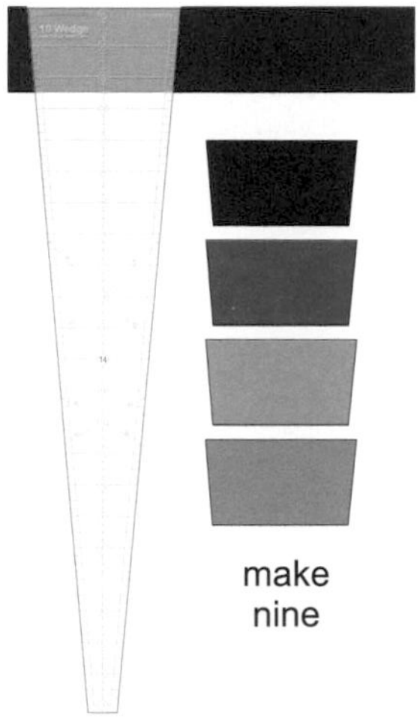

1. From the 2 ½" strips and the wide end of the wedge tool, cut *nine* from each fabric.
2. Fold an edging piece in half, right sides together.
3. Sew across the wide end.
4. Turn the sewn piece to the outside.
5. Open to form a point. Center the seam and press.
6. Repeat for the remaining pieces.
7. Match raw edges, aligning a point to each wedge. Pin and sew around the edge of the circle.

Creative Option

Double the points for added interest. Make twice as many folded points.

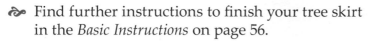

- Find further instructions to finish your tree skirt in the *Basic Instructions* on page 56.

Changing the Tree Skirt Size

All sizes below use four fabrics: A,B,C,and D

25" Speedy Spiral

Cut ***eight*** strips 1 ¾" wide from each fabric. Suggested yardage is ½ yard per fabric. Use the Mini Ten Degree Wedge template for this project found on page 61. If you cut the wedges carefully, rotating the wedge tool to cut one up and one down, you can make two circles.

50" Speedy Spiral

Cut ***twelve*** strips 3 ¼" wide from each fabric. Make one and a half strip sets. Suggested yardage is 1 ½ yards per fabric.

60" Speedy Spiral

Cut ***eighteen*** strips 2 ¾" wide from each fabric. Make one and a half strip sets of twelve strips of fabric in the same sequence as shown on page 21. Suggested yardage is 1 ⅝ yards per fabric.

The 60" size requires joining the Ten Degree Wedge to the Ten Degree Wedge Extension found on page 63. Use the 30" line on the extension to make the folded edging pieces.

70" Speedy Spiral

Cut **24** strips 3 ¼" wide from each fabric. Make two strip set of 12 strips of fabric in the same sequence as shown on page 63. Suggested yardage is 2 ¼ yards per fabric.

The 70" size requires joining the Ten Degree Wedge to the Ten Degree Wedge Extension found on page 63. Use the wide end of the extension to make the folded edging pieces.

Creative Options

Changing Sizes

(Photographs are in scale with each other)

Chained Melody Variation

with solid wedges

25 inch circle

Page 46

Windmill Swirl

50 inch circle

Page 16

Speedy Spiral Variation

70 inch circle

Page 22

Butterfly Reborn

Be sure to read over both the introduction, pages 4 and 5 and the basic instructions, page 54 to 57 before beginning your project.

Finished Circle
50" in diameter

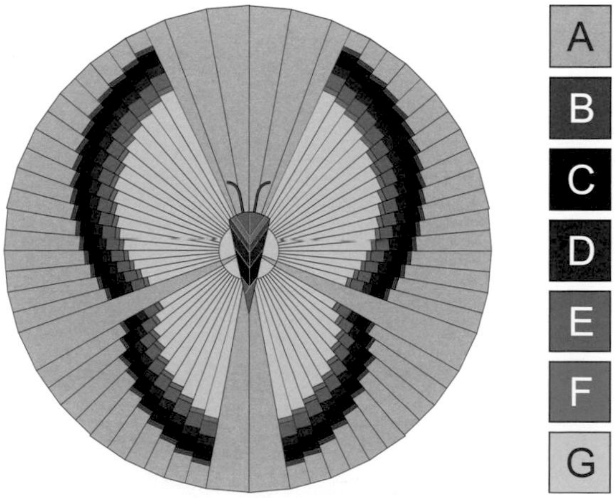

Fabric

Color A	2 yd	[63" actual]
Color B	3/8 yd	[11" actual]
Color C	1/2 yd	[12" actual]
Color D	1/3 yd	[9" actual]
Color E	1/2 yd	[12" actual]
Color F	1/4 yd	[6" actual]
Color G	2 3/8 yd	[78" actual]
Binding	1/2 yd	
Backing	3 yd	
Batting	54" x 54"	

Overview of the Butterfly

1. *Sew strip sets.*
2. *Sub-cut into set strips.*
3. *Make offset panels.*
4. *Cut wedges from the panels.*
5. *Sew wedges into half circles.*
6. *Add butterfly body.*
7. *Sew halves into circle.*

Cutting

Cut Strips in the widths as shown below.

Color A

One strip ....24 1/2" x width
Two strips ....11" x width
One strip ....7 1/2" x width
One strip ....5 1/2" x width
One strip ....3 1/2" x width

Color B

One piece** .... 5" x 7"
Six strips* ....1" x width

Color C

Six strips* .... 2" x width

Color D

Six strips* ....1 1/2" x width

Color E

Six strips* .... 2" x width

Color F

Six strips* ....1" x width

Color G

One strip .... 17" x width
Two strips ....15" x width
Two strips ....12" x width
One piece* .... 7" x 8"

** Set aside one strip from B - F for the Butterfly body*
*** Set aside for antennae*

Step One Sewing the Strip Sets

*Sew **exact** ¼" seams through out.*

Strip Sets 1-4

1. Sew each strip set.
2. Press seam allowances toward the A strip.
3. Fold the strip set in half, right sides together, then sub-cut each strip set into 3" wide vertical strips.

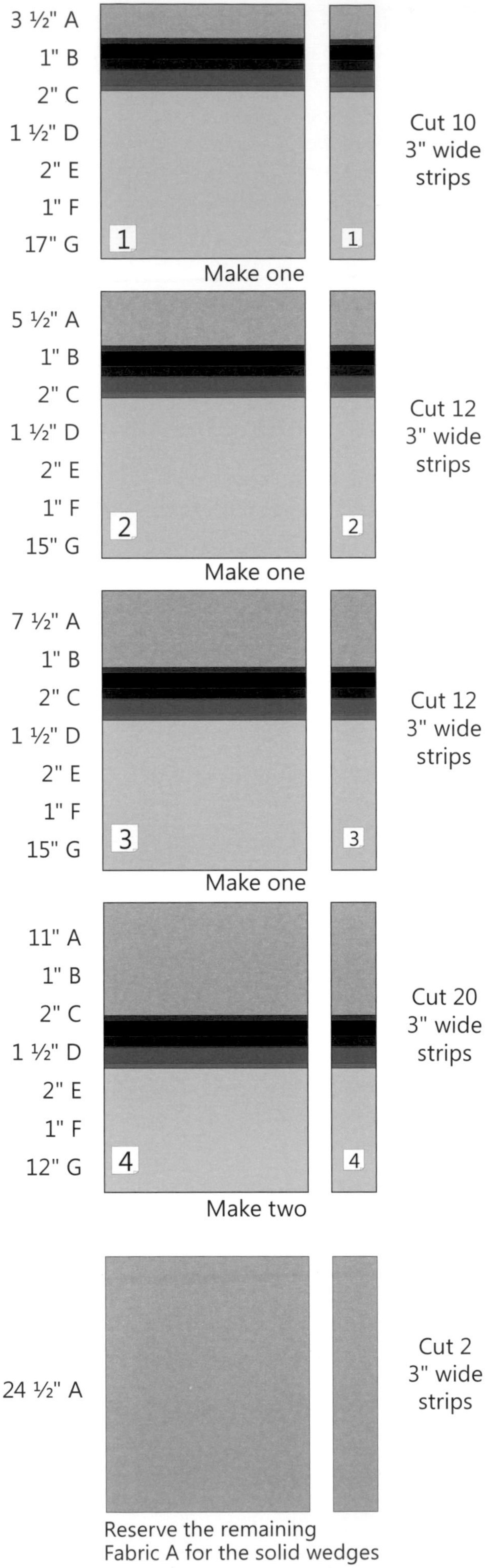

Panels

Panels are two **set strips** offset, then sewn together.

The offset measurement refers to the strip placed on the top, shown as the right side of the panel.

Offset set strips for the **right upper** wing and the **left lower** wing by stepping ***down***.

Offset set strips for the **left upper** wing and the **right lower** wing by stepping ***up***.

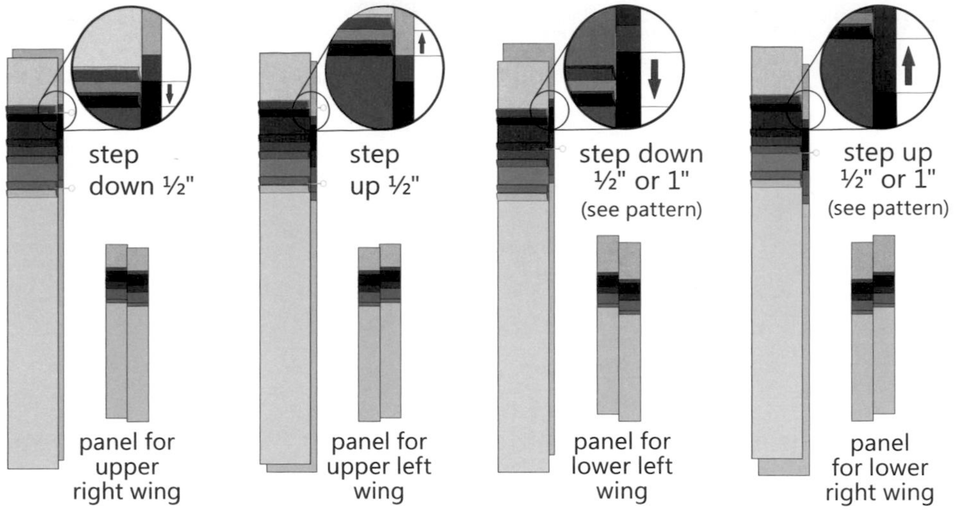

Step Two   Cutting the Wedges

- Prepare the wedge tool as described on page 54.
- Use the ***upper*** A/B seam for alignment to the wedge line indicated.

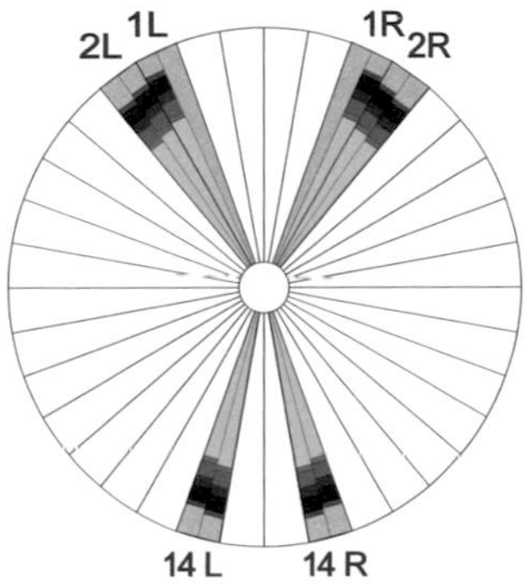

wedge placement

Set 1 Panels

Use Set 1 panels to make the six wedges shown in the placement diagram.

Wedges 1L and 1R

1. Sew a 3" strip of fabric A to the ***right*** side of a Set 1 piece.
2. Center the wedge tool to the Set 1 piece, aligning the A/B seam with the 23 ½" line.
3. Cut the wedge. Label 1L.
4. Sew a 3" strip of fabric A to the ***left*** side of a Set 1 piece.
5. Center the wedge tool to the Set 1 piece, aligning the A/B seam with the 23 ½" line.
6. Cut the wedge. Label 1R.

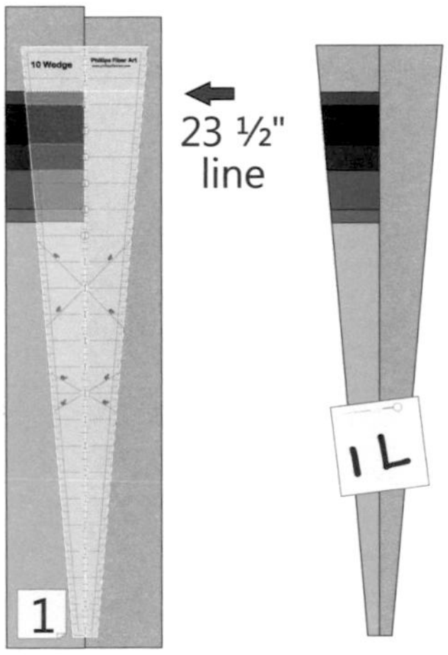

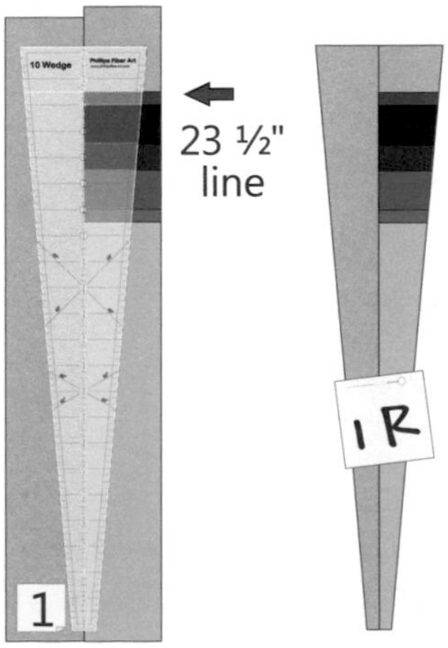

Wedges 2L, 2R, 14L and 14R

1. Offset the top Set 1 piece stepping ***up*** ½" and sew together.
2. Cut two wedges aligning the A/B seam to the 23" line. Label 2L and 14R.

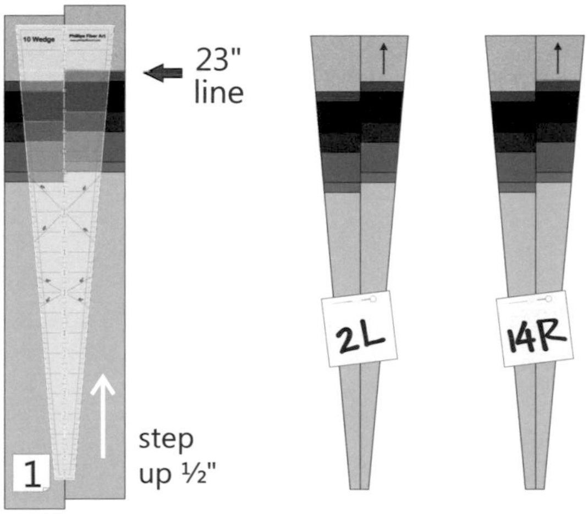

3. Offset the top Set 1 piece stepping ***down*** ½" and sew together.
4. Cut two wedges aligning the A/B seam to the 23" line. Label 2R and 14L.

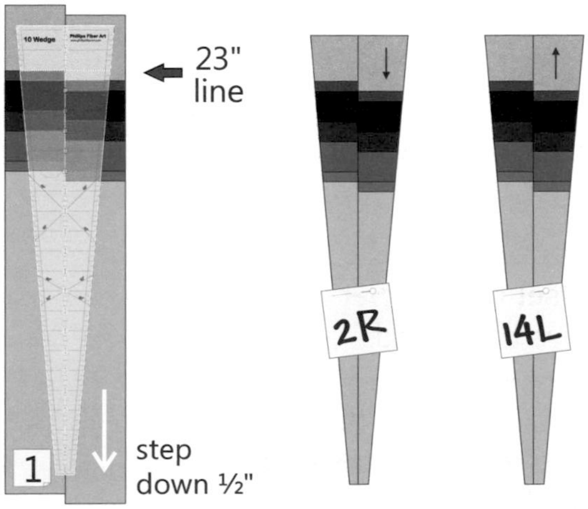

Strip Set 2

Use Set 2 panels to make the six wedges shown in the placement diagram.

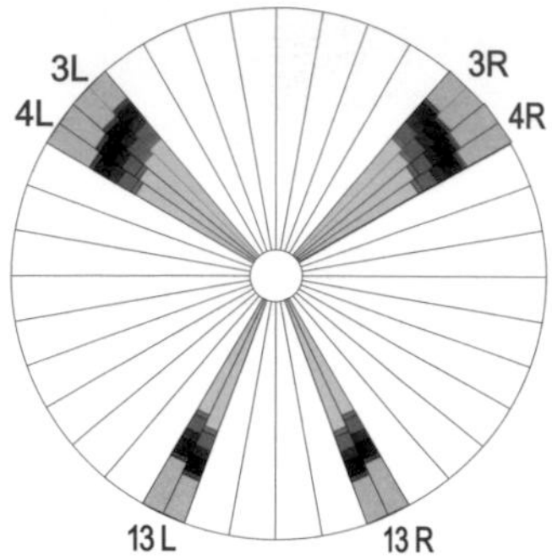

wedge placement

Wedge 3L

Offset the top Set 2 piece ***up*** ½" and sew together. Align with the 22" line. Cut the wedge. Label 3L.

Wedge 3R

Offset the top Set 2 piece ***down*** ½" and sew together. Align seam A/B with the 22" line. Cut the wedge. Label 3R.

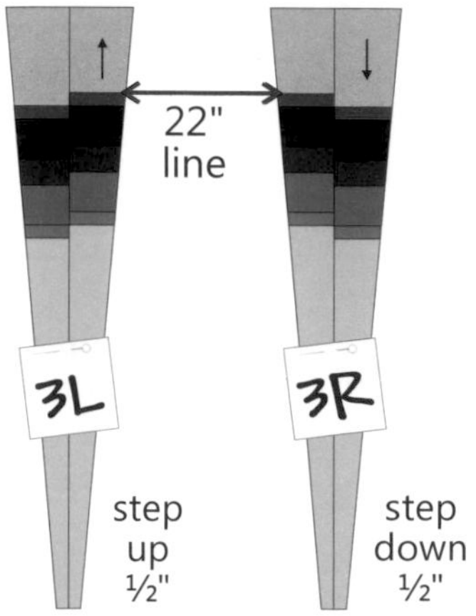

Wedge 4L

Offset the top Set 2 piece ***up*** ½" and sew together. Align with the 21" line. Cut the wedge. Label 4L.

Wedge 4R

Offset the top Set 2 piece ***down*** ½" and sew together. Align seam A/B with the 21" line. Cut the wedge. Label 4R.

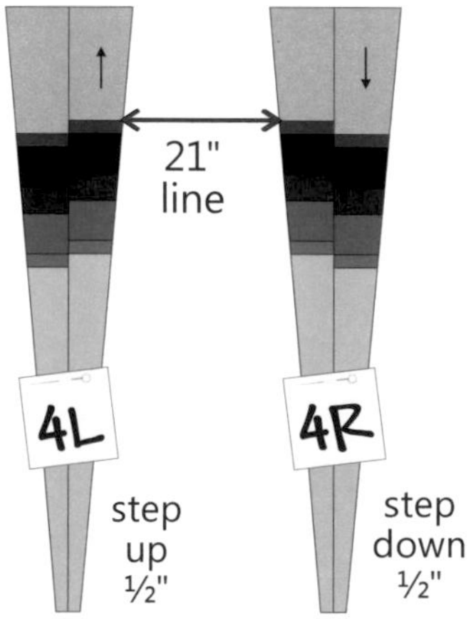

Wedge 13L

Offset the top Set 2 piece ***down*** **1**" and sew together. Align seam A/B with the 22" line. Cut the wedge. Label 13L.

Wedge 13R

Offset the top Set 2 piece ***up*** **1**" and sew together. Align seam A/B with the 22" line. Cut the wedge. Label 13R.

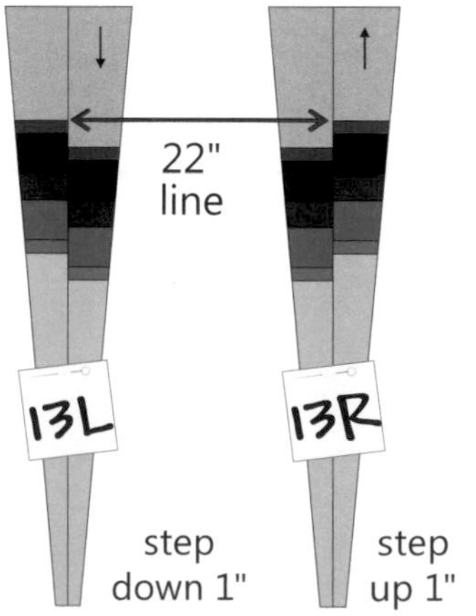

Strip Set 3

Use Set 3 panels to make the six wedges shown in the placement diagram.

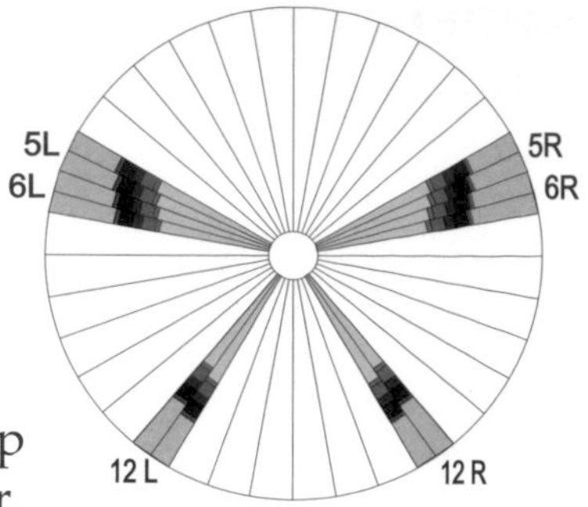

wedge placement

Wedge 5L

Offset the top Set 3 strip ***up*** ½" and sew together. Align seam A/B with the 20" line. Cut the wedge. Label 5L.

Wedge 5R

Offset the top Set 3 strip ***down*** ½" and sew together. Align seam A/B with the 20" line. Cut the wedge. Label 5R.

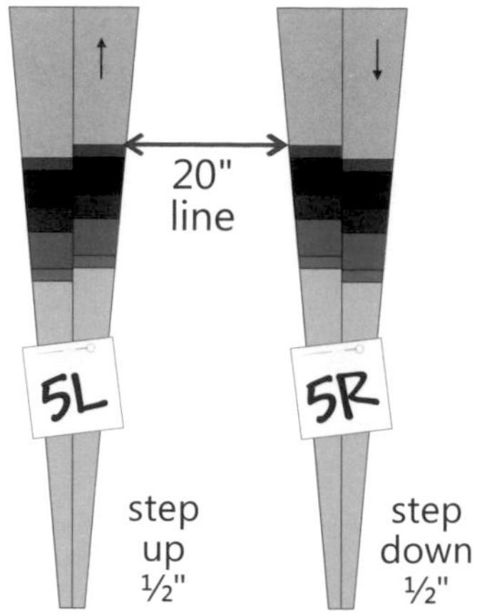

Wedge 6L

Offset the top Set 3 strip ***up*** ½" and sew together. Align seam A/B with the 19" line. Cut the wedge. Label 6L.

Wedge 6R

Offset the top Set 3 strip ***down*** ½" and sew together. Align seam A/B with the 19" line. Cut the wedge. Label 6R.

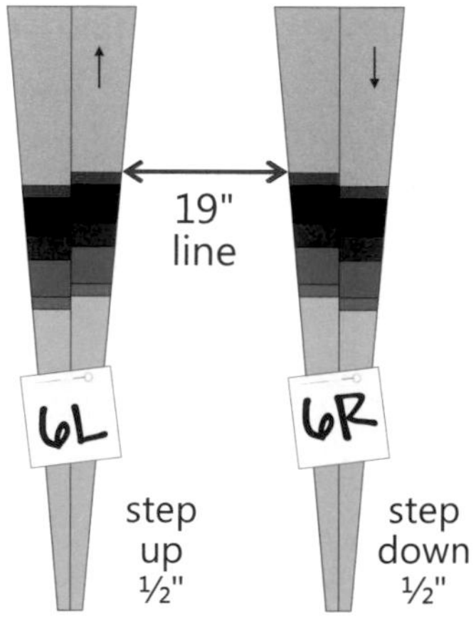

Wedge 12L

Offset the top Set 3 strip ***down*** **1**" and sew together. Align seam A/B with the 20" line. Cut the wedge. Label 12L.

Wedge 12R

Offset the top Set 3 strip ***up*** **1**" and sew together. Align seam A/B with the 20" line. Cut the wedge. Label 12R.

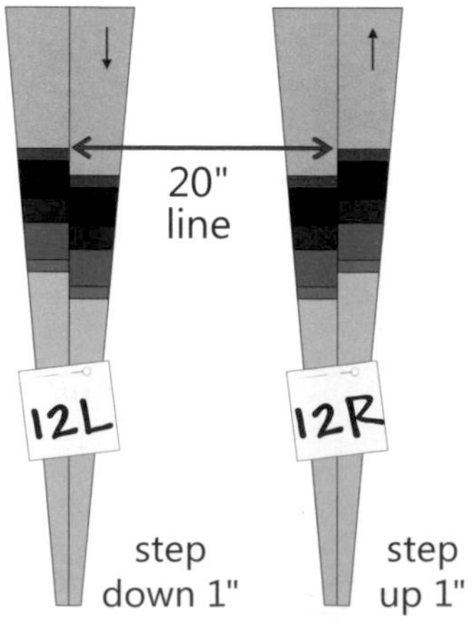

Strip Set 4

Use Set 4 panels to make the eight wedges shown in the placement diagram.

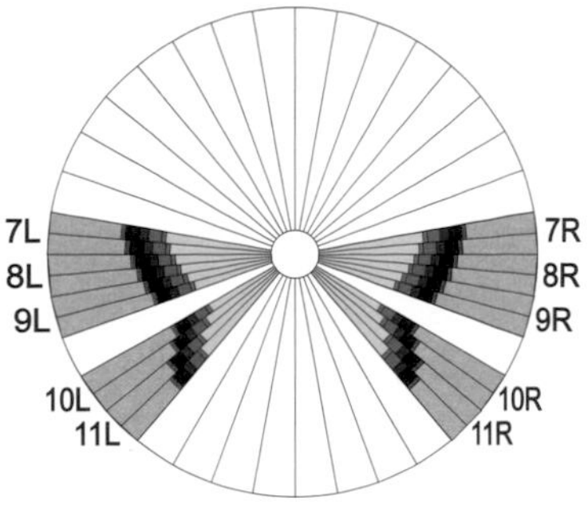

wedge placement

Wedge 7L

Offset the top Set 4 strip ***up*** ½" and sew together. Align seam A/B with the 18" line. Cut the wedge. Label 7L.

Wedge 7R

Offset the top Set 4 strip ***down*** ½" and sew together. Align seam A/B with the 18" line. Cut the wedge. Label 7R.

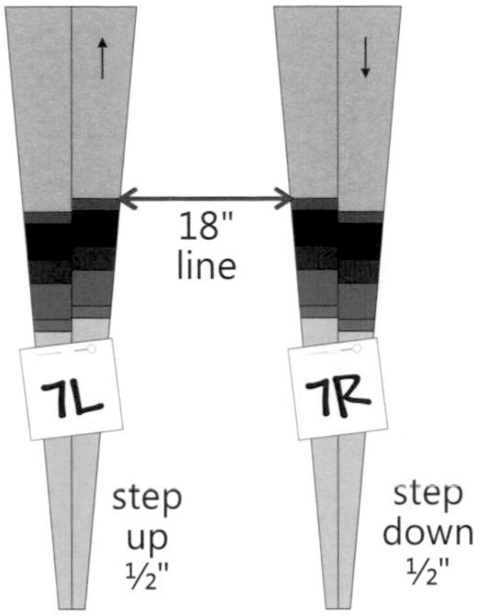

Wedge 8L

Offset the top Set 4 strip ***up*** ½" and sew together. Align seam A/B with thc 17" line. Cut the wedge. Label 8L.

Wedge 8R

Offset the top Set 4 strip ***down*** ½" and sew together. Align seam A/B the 17" line. Cut the wedge. Label 8R.

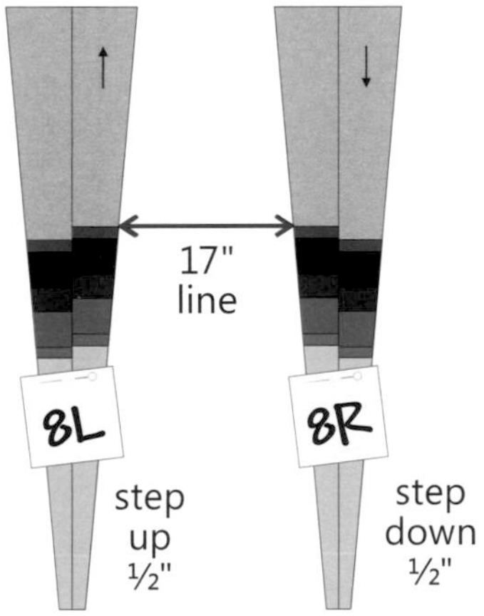

Wedge 9L

Offset the top Set 4 strip ***up*** ½" and sew together. Align seam A/B with the 16" line. Cut the wedge. Label 9L.

Wedge 9R

Offset the top Set 4 strip ***down*** ½" and sew together. Align seam A/B with the 16" line. Cut the wedge. Label 9R.

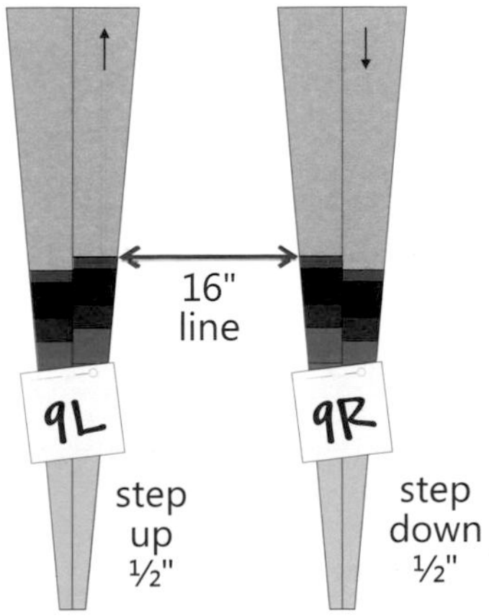

Wedge 11L

Offset the top Set 4 strip ***down*** **1**" and sew together. Align seam A/B with the 18" line. Cut the wedge. Label 11L.

Wedge 11R

Offset the top Set 4 strip ***up*** **1**" and sew together. Align seam A/B with the 18" line. Cut the wedge. Label 11R.

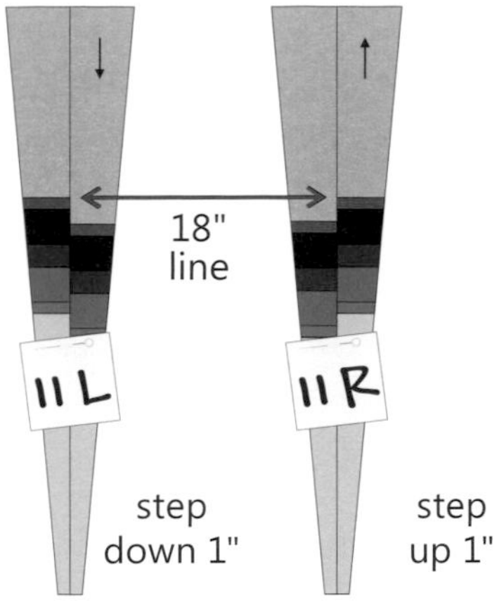

Wedge 10L

Offset the top Set 4 strip ***down*** **1**" and sew together. Align seam A/B with the 16" line. Cut the wedge. Label 10L.

Wedge 10R

Offset the top Set 4 strip ***up*** **1**" and sew together. Align seam A/B with the 16" line. Cut the wedge. Label 10R.

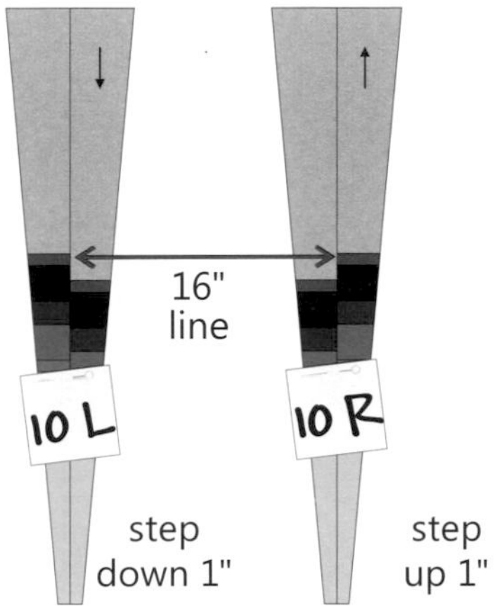

Solid Wedges

Cut eight butterfly wedges from the remaining strip of Fabric A as shown here.

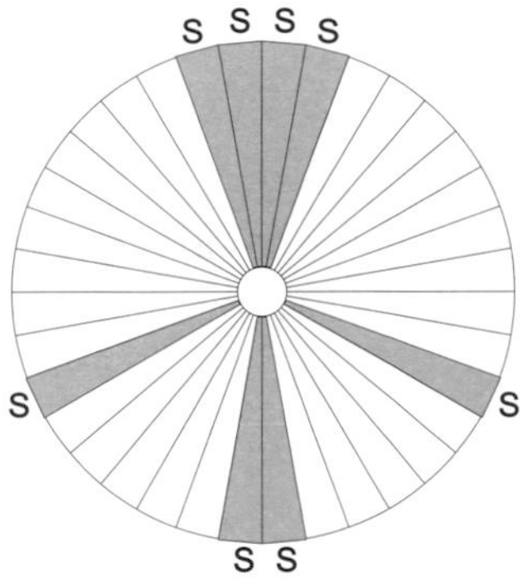

wedge placement

S Wedges

Cut **eight** solid wedges from the remaining Fabric A strip. Label S.

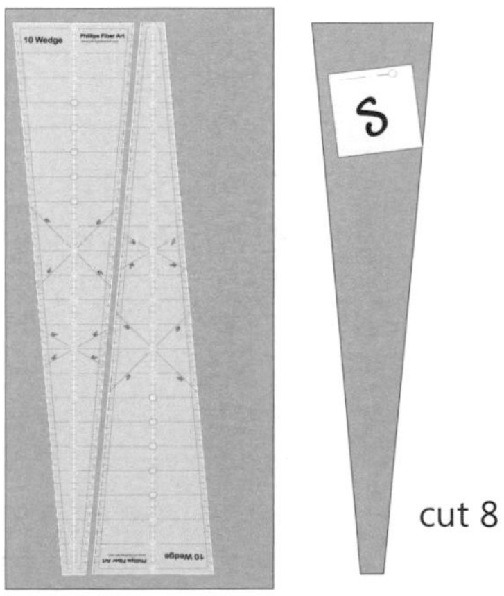

Step Three Constructing the Circle

Sewing Halves

Sew wedges in the order shown below to make two halves.

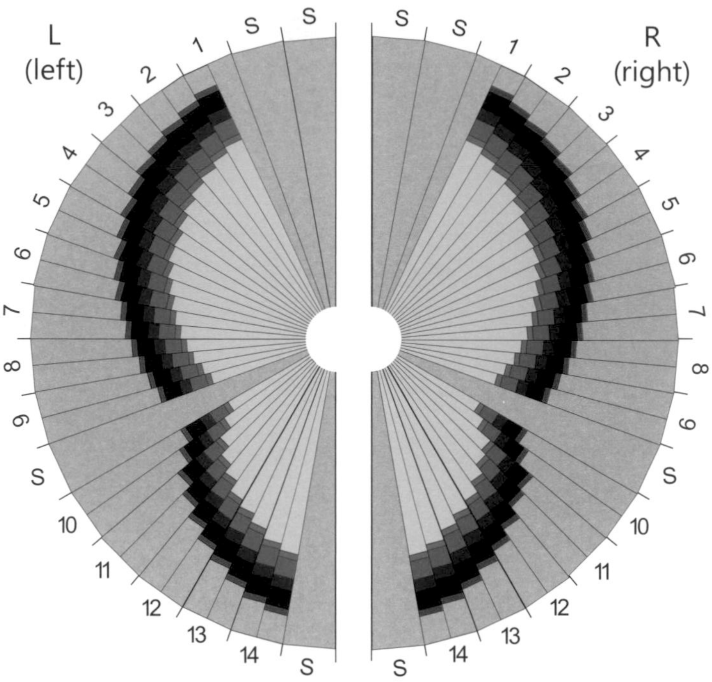

Preparing the Center

Stabilize the center openings

1. Lay the butterfly, wrong side up, on your pressing surface.
2. Using the half circle template found on page 61 as a guide, adjust the half circle opening to make them the same size and equally round.
3. Iron a piece of freezer paper to the wrong side of the center opening to stabilize the shape of the opening.
4. Measure the half circle diameter.
5. Repeat for the other side.

Find tips on Pressing on page 55.

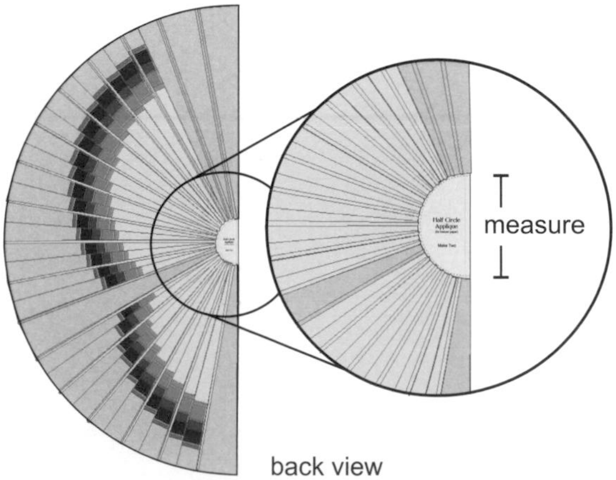

back view

Half Circle Appliques

- *You have two choices for the center half appliques: make the half circles from Fabric G or piece the half circles with wedges of Fabrics G and A.*
- *Some fabric choices, such as linear designs or those with strong contrast to the background, are better suited to a pieced half circle applique.*

The choice is yours.

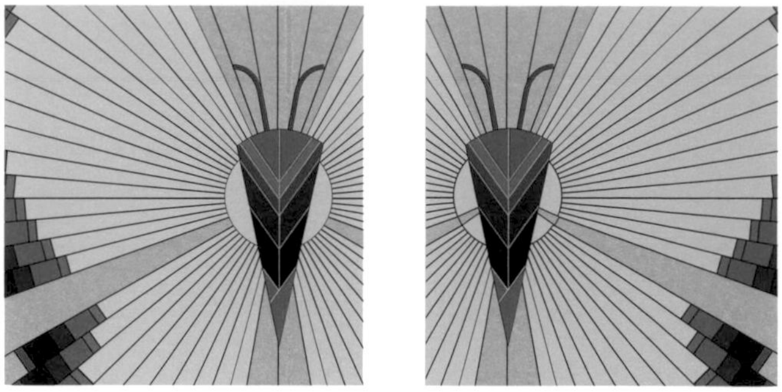

with solid half circles — with pieced half circles

Optional Pieced Half Circle Appliques

1. Trace the lines onto the Mini 30 Degree Wedge template, see page 61.
2. Cut a 3 ½" strip of Fabric G.
3. Cut ***ten*** mini 30 degree wedges from the 3 ½" strip.
4. Cut a 1 ¾" x 7 ½" strip from the remaining Fabric G.
5. Cut a 1 ¼" x 7 ½" strip of Fabric A.
6. Sew the 7 ½" strips of Fabrics A and G together.

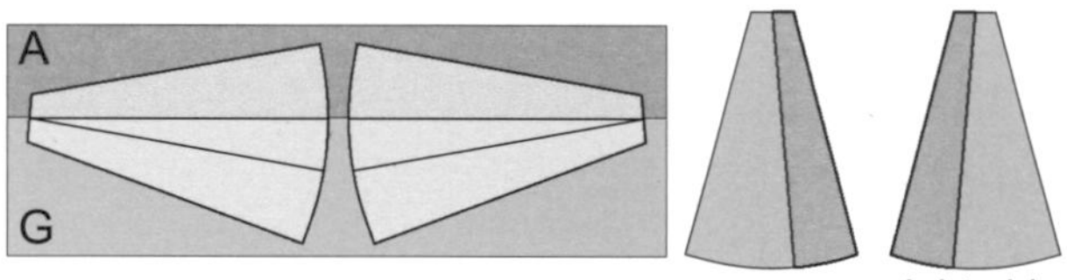

7. Place the Mini 30 Degree Wedge template onto the A/G strip set, aligning the marked line to the seam, and cut ***one*** fabric wedge.
8. Rotate the mini wedge aligning the other marked line to the A/G seam, cut ***one*** fabric wedge.
9. Sew five solid and one pieced mini wedge to make the left half circle applique. Repeat for the right side.
10. Use the pieced half circles to create half circle appliques on the next page.

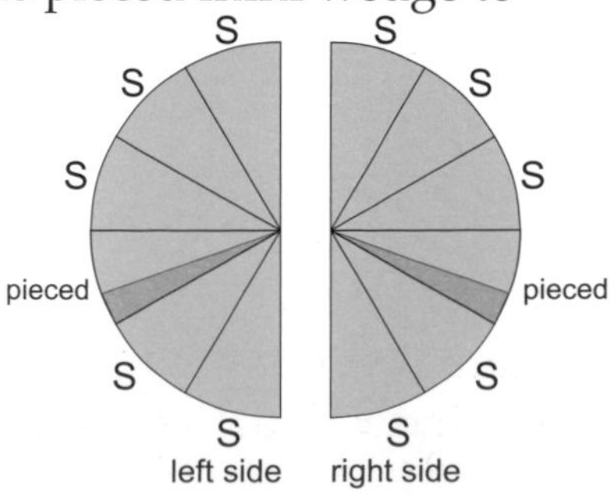

Half Circle Appliques

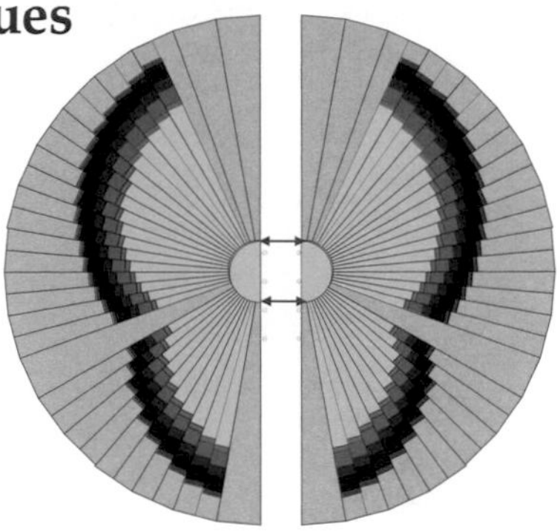

1. Trace two half circle appliques onto freezer paper ½" larger than the half circle measurement. See page 61 for template
2. Make half circle appliques as shown on page 61 using Fabric G or the pieced half circles from the previous page.
3. Lay out the two butterfly halves side by side.
4. Pin the half circle appliques over the openings aligning one with the other.
5. Applique the center half circles.
6 Leave the freezer paper attached until the body is inserted.

Making the Butterfly Body

Chevron

1. Trace the two butterfly body templates found on page 62 onto freezer paper.
2. Cut the remaining B-F strips into 20" lengths.
3. Sew one strip set.
4. Press the seams open.

5. Fold the strip set in half, right sides together.
6. Match and pin at the seam intersections.
7. Align the template edge to the Fabric C strip with the lines parallel to the seams
8. Iron the chevron template onto the strip set as shown.
9. Sew directly next to the edge of the freezer paper.

10. Open the fabric and check for matching seams. If not, adjust the intersections.

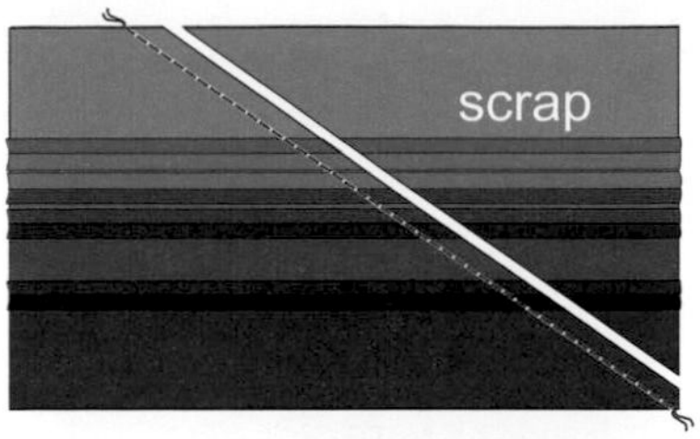

11. When seams match, trim approximately ¼" from the stitching. Remove the freezer paper.
12. Press the seam open.

Tail

1. Cut two 3" x 8" pieces from Fabric E.
2. Sew a strip on the left side of the chevron piece, with right sides together.
3. Open and press the seam allowances open.
4. Trim Strip E even with the left side as shown.

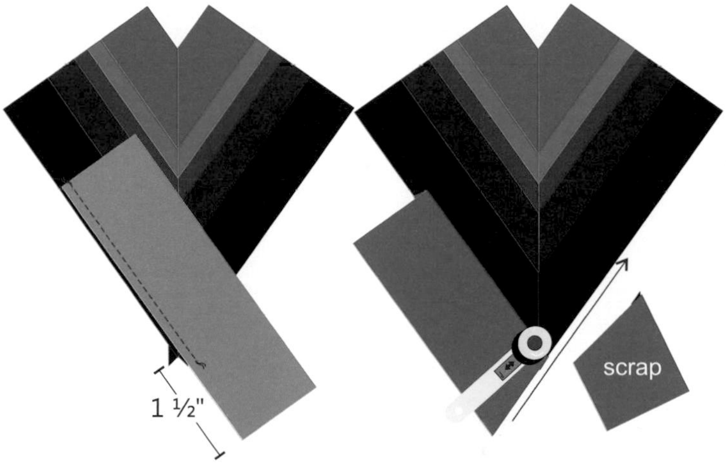

5. Sew the second strip to the right side of the chevron piece.
6. Press the seam open.

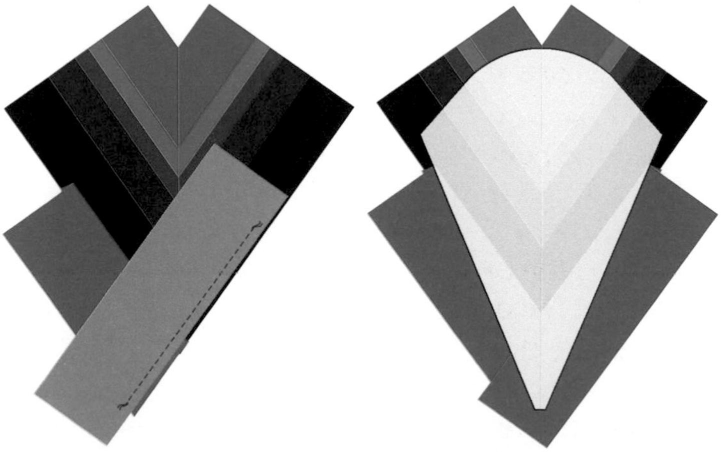

7. Center the fold of the freezer paper template to the seam and press to the fabric.

8. Cut out the butterfly body piece carefully.
9. Cut a facing from Fabric B using the template found on page 62.
10. Sew the facing to the top of the butterfly body.
11. Turn the facing the back side of the body piece.
12. Fold the body piece in half, ***wrong*** sides together.

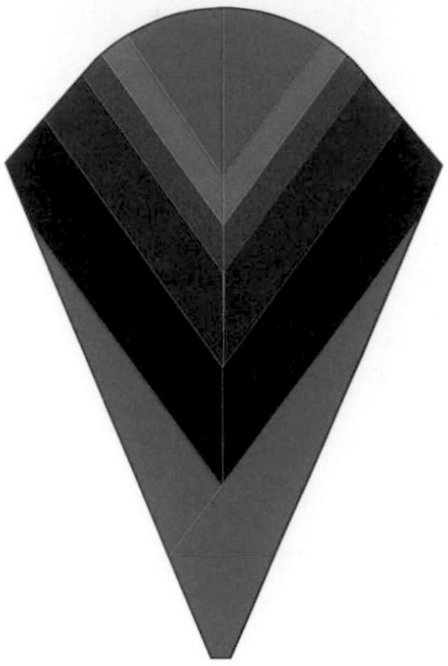

Inserting the Body Piece

1. Pin the folded butterfly body 1 ½" below the circle appliqué on the left butterfly half.

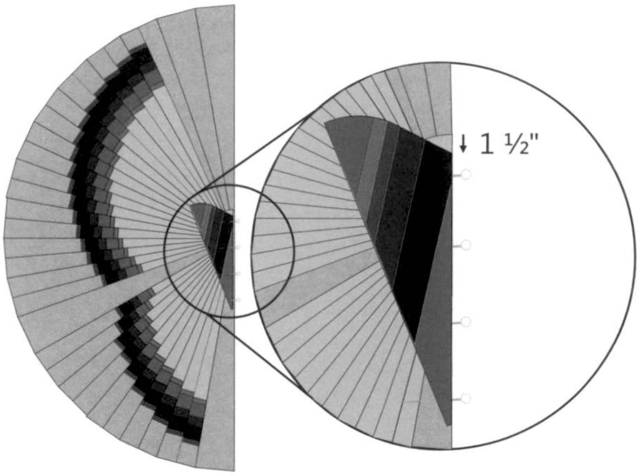

2. Place the right half on top, making sure the edges of the circle appliqués match.
3. Pin along the length of the center seam.
4. Sew the two halves together, sandwiching the butterfly body between the halves.
5. Press the seam open, keeping the butterfly body to one side.
6. From the front side, open the butterfly body. Align the center seam of the body to the center seam of the quilt.
7. Shape the tip with your fingers before pressing. Carefully press toward the top of the body, moving the iron away from the tip.

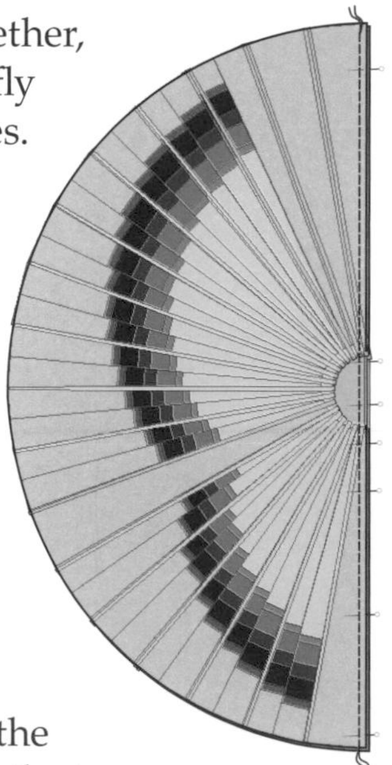

Adding Antennae

1. Cut two 1" x 6" bias strips from the 5" x 7" piece of Fabric B.
2. Fold the end of the strip over
3. Fold a strip in half with wrong sides together.
4. Sew with a scant ¼" seam.
5. Center the seam allowance to the tube and press.
6. Repeat for the other antennae.
7. Shape the bias strips using the antennae pattern found on page 62.

   Press to hold shape.
8. Applique the antennae following the wedge seams to the right and left of the center seam.

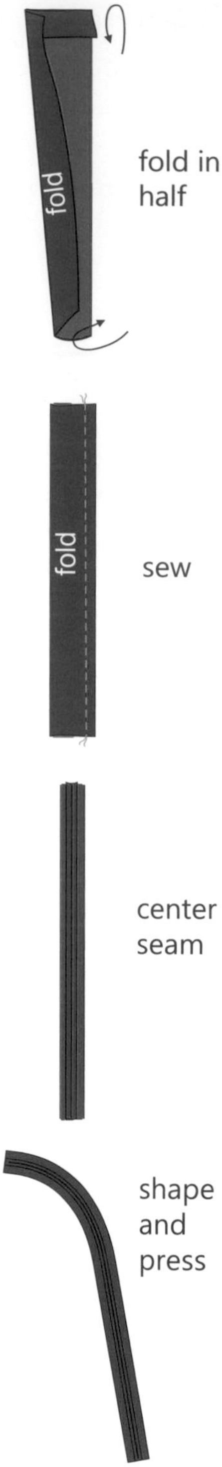

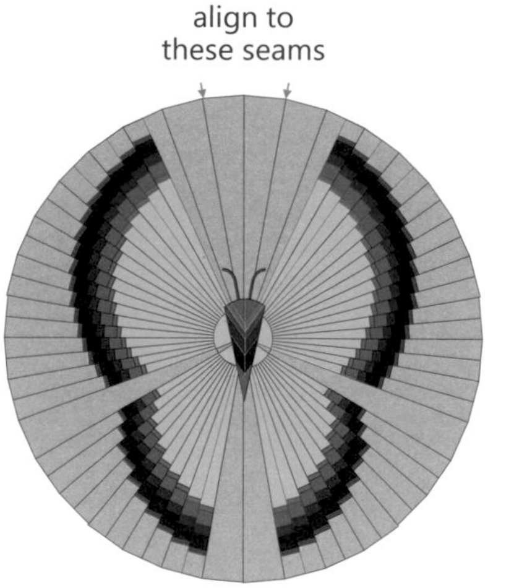

Applique the Body

Applique the curved top of the butterfly body and the sides of the body. Stitching the sides is optional as the butterfly body is securely sewn into the center seam.

Step Four Finishing

The Butterfly quilt top is now ready for the finishing process. You will find the help you need in the *Basic Instructions* on page 56.

Chained Melody
Page 41

Bargello in the Round
Page 9

Butterfly Reborn
Page 24

Speedy Spiral
Page 20

Chained Melody Variation
Page 46

Butterfly Reborn
Page 24

Butterfly Reborn
Page 24

Butterfly Reborn
Page 24

Jazzy Jolt
Page 24

Jazzy Jolt

Be sure to read over both the introduction, pages 4 and 5 and the basic instructions, page 54 to 57 before beginning your project.

Finished Size

50" in diameter

Fabric

Color A	7/8 yd	[24" actual]
Color B	7/8 yd	[24" actual]
Color C	7/8 yd	[24" actual]
Color D	7/8 yd	[24" actual]
Color E	7/8 yd	[24" actual]
Color F	7/8 yd	[24" actual]
Binding	1/2 yd	
Backing	3 yd	
Batting	54" x 54"	

Cutting

- Cut Strips in the widths as shown below.
- Group and label the strips according to width and color.

Colors A-F

From each fabric cut:

Two Strips each..........................3 1/2" x width
One Strip each............................4 1/2" x width
One Strip each............................5 1/2" x width
One Strip each............................6 1/2" x width

Step One Sewing the Strip Sets

- *Sew **exact** ¼" seams through out.*
- *Label all strip sets as shown.*

Strip Sets 1-6

1. Offset each strip as shown below. Begin sewing with the widest strip.
2. Sew Strip Set 1 in order.
3. Repeat for Strip Sets 2-6 as shown.

- *Press seam allowances toward the widest strip.*

Offset strips to provide the best use of fabric.

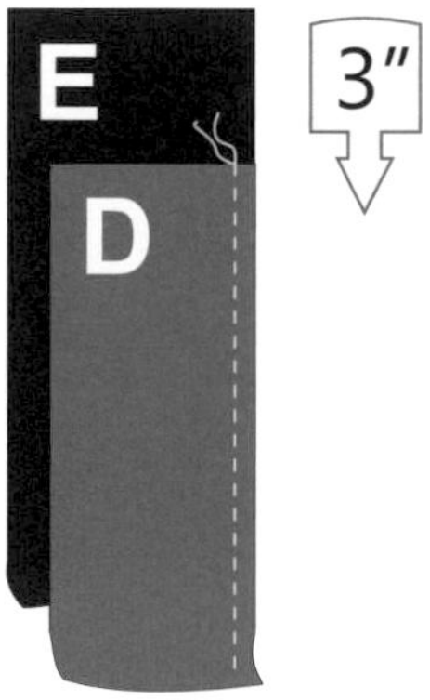

Example: Strip Set 1, place the D Strip 3" from the top of the E Strip.

Step Two Cutting the Wedges

- Trace the additional 60 degree lines shown in red onto your wedge tool. The additional lines are parallel to the 60 degree line found on the tool.
- Prepare the wedge tool following the instructions on page 54.
- Always place the narrow end of the wedge on the narrow strip.

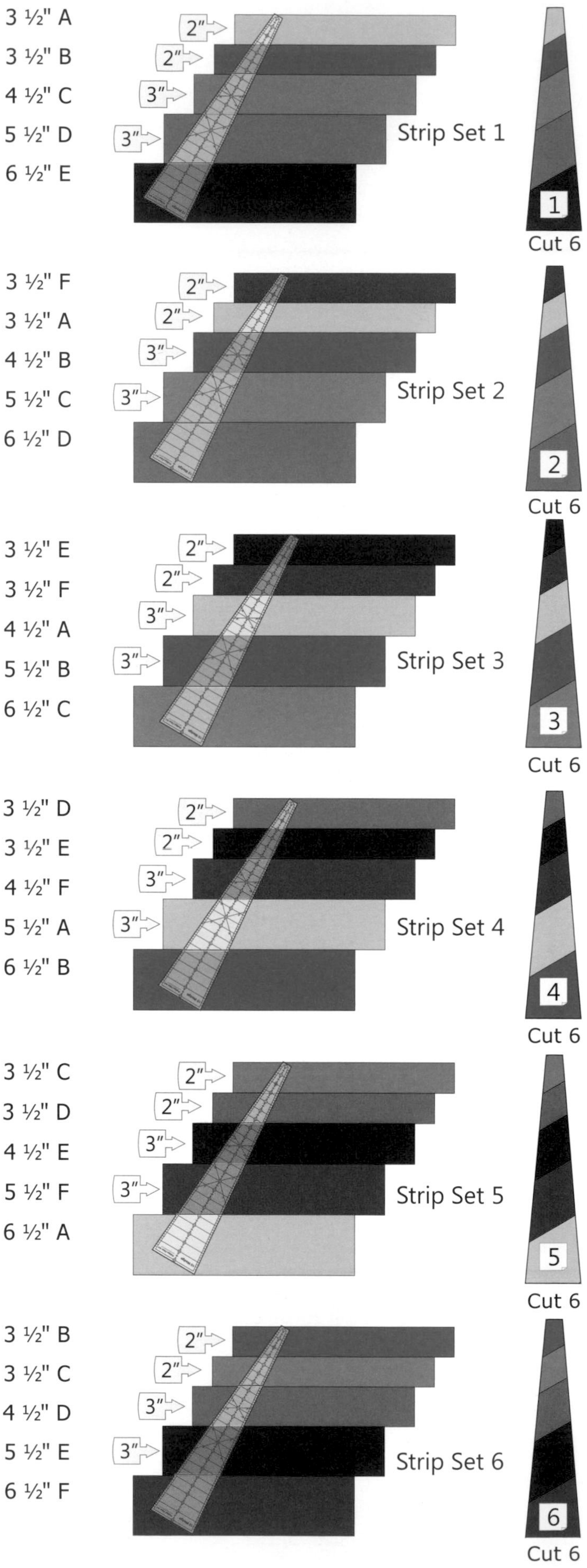

Strip Sets 1-6

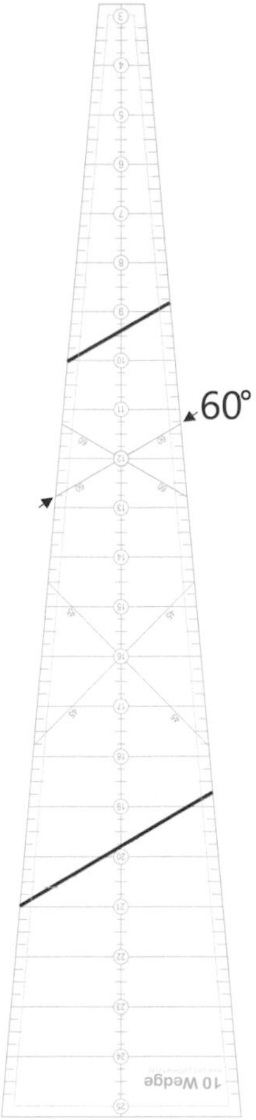

1. Place the marked wedge lines on seams B/C and D/E of Strip Set 1.
   Cut ***six*** wedges. Label as #1.
2. Place the marked wedge lines on seams A/B and C/D of Strip set 2.
   Cut ***six*** wedges. Label as #2.
3. Place the marked wedge lines on seams F/A and B/C of Strip Set 3.
   Cut ***six*** wedges. Label as #3.
4. Place the marked wedge lines on seams E/F and A/B of Strip Set 4.
   Cut ***six*** wedges. Label as #4.
5. Place the marked wedge lines on seams D/E and F/A of Strip Set 5.
   Cut ***six*** wedges. Label as #5.
6. Place the marked wedge lines on seams C/D and E/F of Strip Set 6.
   Cut ***six*** wedges. Label as #6.

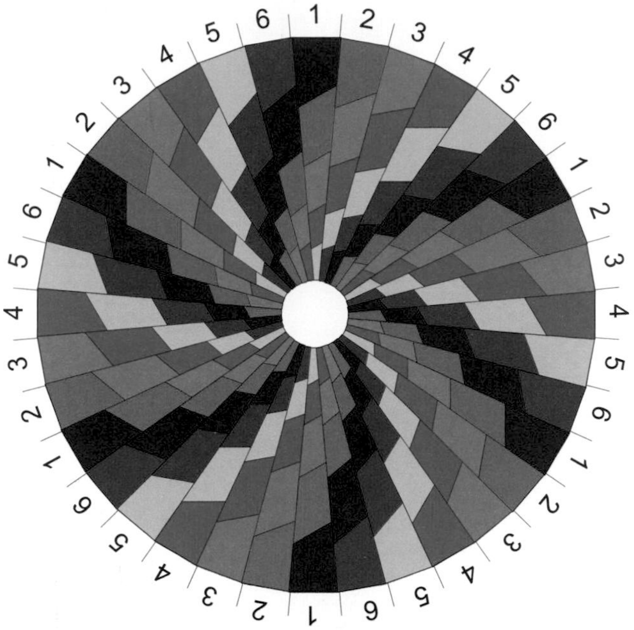

Step Three Constructing the Circle

Sewing Wedges

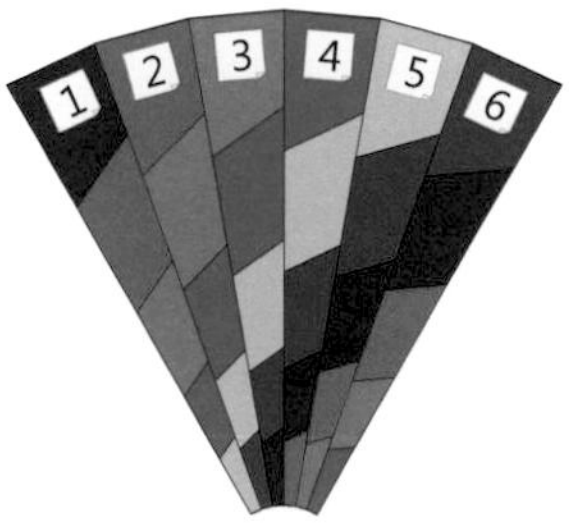

1. Lay out ***six*** wedges in order.
2. Sew the ***six*** wedges together.
3. Repeat for the remaining wedges for ***six*** units.
4. Sew the units into a circle.
3. Press after the top is complete.

Find tips on Pressing on page 55.

Center Applique

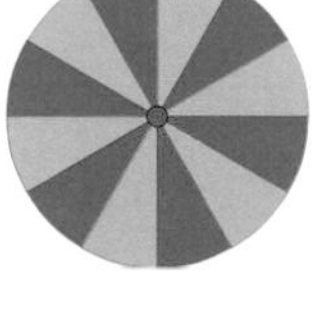

1. Trace the Mini 30 Degree Wedge found on page 61 onto template plastic.
2. Using scrap pieces, cut ***six*** small wedges of both Fabrics A and D.
3. Sew the wedges to make a circle.
4. Refer to the *Pieced Center Appliqué* instructions found on page 56.

You may substitute a coordinating motif or one of the main fabrics as your center applique.

Step Four Finishing

The Jazzy Jolt quilt top is now ready for the finishing process. You will find the help you need in the *Basic Instructions* on page 56.

Making a 25" Jazzy Jolt

Refer to the basic pattern for detailed instructions.

Use the Mini Ten Degree Wedge template found on page 61. If using an acrylic Mini Ten Degree tool, trace the 60 degree markings onto the tool following the lines found on page 61.
Suggested yardage for each fabric is ¼ yard.
Cut half width strips: 1 ½", 2", 2 ½", 3", and 3 ½".
Make ***six*** strip sets, offsetting each strip by 1".
Assemble following the pattern instructions.
Applique the center using the same sized circle used for the full size version.

Creative Options

Be a "fabric chef"...
Start with the quilt recipe,
add ingredients and mix it up to make it your own
one of a kind creation.
Just have fun!

Change the Order

Simply change the order of the wedges to get *floating diamonds*. These are the same wedges used in the basic pattern.

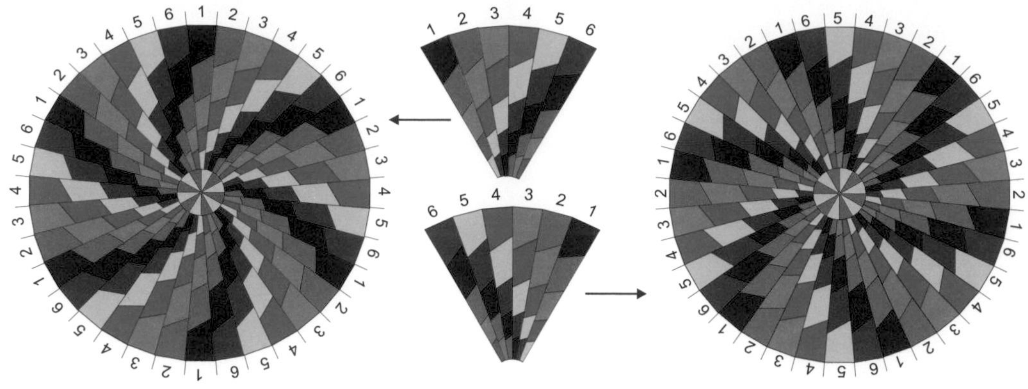

as shown in pattern

change in wedge order

Fabric Selection

Higher contrast between the fabrics places more focus on the design.

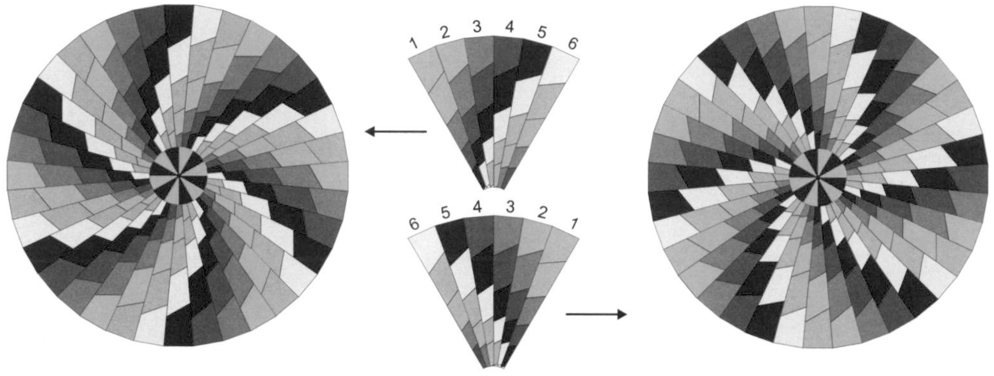

as shown in pattern

change in wedge order

A Different Twist

Reversing the wedge placement on the strip sets changes the arc of the Jazzy Jolt lines. Place the wide end of the wedge on the narrower strips and the narrow end of the wedge on the wider strips as shown

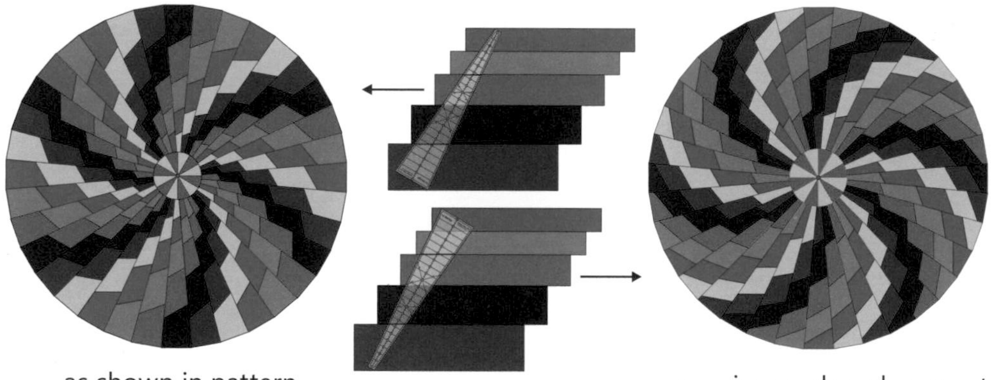

as shown in pattern

reversing wedge placement

Take it Further

Higher contrasting fabric emphasizes the design. Reversing wedge order offers another variation.

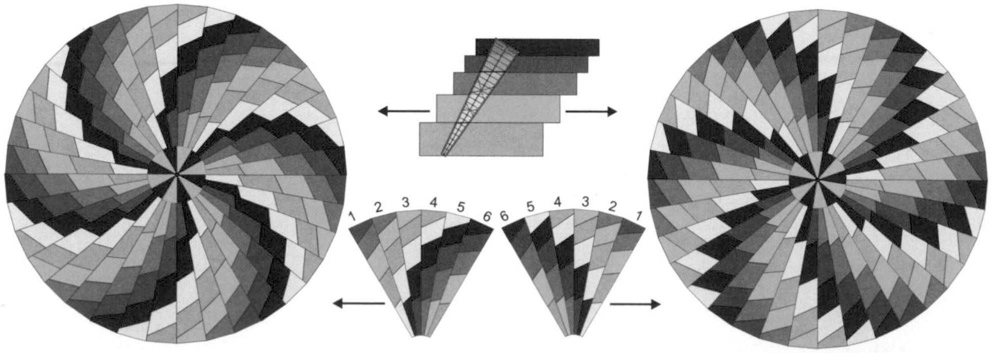

reversing wedge placement

reversed wedge with change in wedge order

This page is only intended to inspire. You'll want to make the pattern before trying variations.

Chained Melody

Be sure to read over both the introduction, pages 4 and 5, and the basic instructions, page 54 to 57 before beginning your project.

Finished Circle
50" in diameter

Fabric

Color A	1 3/4 yd	[55" actual]
Color B	3/4 yd	[18" actual]
Color C	3/4 yd	[18" actual]
Color D	3/4 yd	[18" actual]
Color E	1 1/2 yd	[41" actual]
Binding	1/2 yd	
Backing	3 yd	
Batting	54" x 54"	

Chained Melody wedges are made of two wedge pieces cut in opposite directions. Apply spray starch and press fabric before cutting to stabilize bias edges.

Cutting

⌘ Cut strips in the widths as shown below.

⌘ Group and label the strips according to width and color.

Color A

Six Strips.................................... 8" x width
One piece .... 7" x 7" square

Color B

Twelve Strips ....1 1/2" x width

Color C

Twelve Strips .... 1 1/2" x width

Color D

Six Strips .... 3" x width

Color E

Six Strips ....6 3/4" x width

Step One   Sewing the Strip Sets

⌘ Sew *exact* 1/4" seams through out.
⌘ Label all strip sets as shown.

Strip Sets 1-4

1. Offset each strip as shown.

2. Sew Strip Set 1 in order.

3. Repeat for Strip Sets 2-4 as shown.

4. Sew *three* strip sets of each group.

5. Press seam allowances open. It's crucial to keep the strip set seams parallel, especially Strip C in Strip Sets 1 and 2.

6. Label each strip set.

Offset strips to provide the best use of fabric.

Example, Strip Set 1:
Place the B Strip 1 1/2" from the top of the C Strip.

Strip Set 1

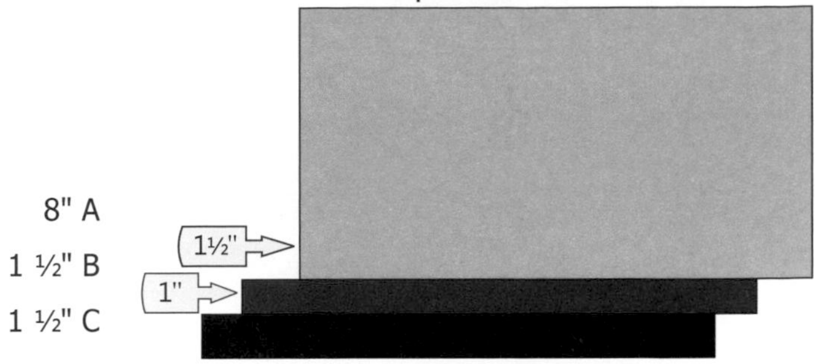

8" A
1 1/2" B
1 1/2" C

1 1/2"
1"

Sew three strip sets

Strip Set 2

8" A
1 1/2" B
1 1/2" C

1 1/2"
1"

Sew three strip sets

Strip Set 3

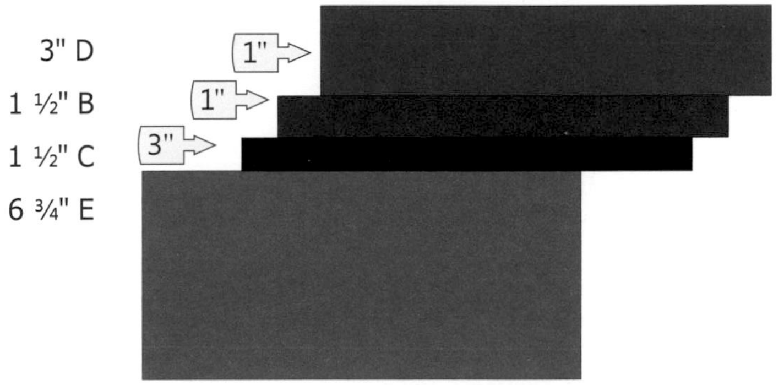

3" D
1 1/2" B
1 1/2" C
6 3/4" E

1"
1"
3"

Sew three strip sets

Strip Set 4

3 D
1 1/2" B
1 1/2" C
6 3/4" E

1"
1"
3"

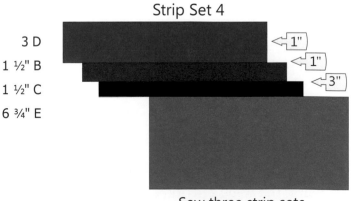

Sew three strip sets

Step Two Cutting the Wedges

⌘ Prepare the wedge tool. See page 54.

Proper preparation is crucial to your success!

⌘ Cut strips with seams aligned to the 45 degree line of the wedge tool.

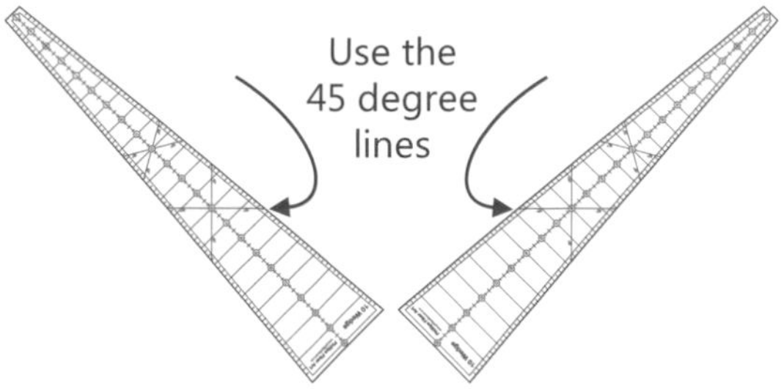

Wedge Pieces 1-2

⌘ *Be sure the edge of Fabric C in Strip Sets 1 & 2 is straight before proceeding. Uneven strips can be the result of uneven cutting, sewing, or pressing. Adjust before proceeding.*

1. Place the wedge tool on Strip Set 1 with the 45 degree line aligned to the edge of Fabric C.

   Cut ***eighteen*** identical wedge pieces, using the narrow portion of the wedge tool.

2. Rotate and place the wedge tool on Strip Set 2 with the opposite 45 degree line aligned to the edge of Fabric C.

   Cut ***eighteen*** identical wedge pieces, using the narrow portion of the wedge tool.

Wedge Pieces 3-4

⌘ *Be sure you allow very little space between the wide end of the wedge and the previous cut in order to have enough fabric.*

1. Place the wedge tool on Strip Set 3 with the 45 degree line aligned to seam D/B.

   Cut ***eighteen*** identical wedge pieces, using the wide portion of the wedge tool.

2. Rotate and place the wedge tool on Strip Set 4 with the opposite 45 degree line aligned to seam D/B.

   Cut ***eighteen*** identical wedge pieces, using the wide portion of the wedge tool.

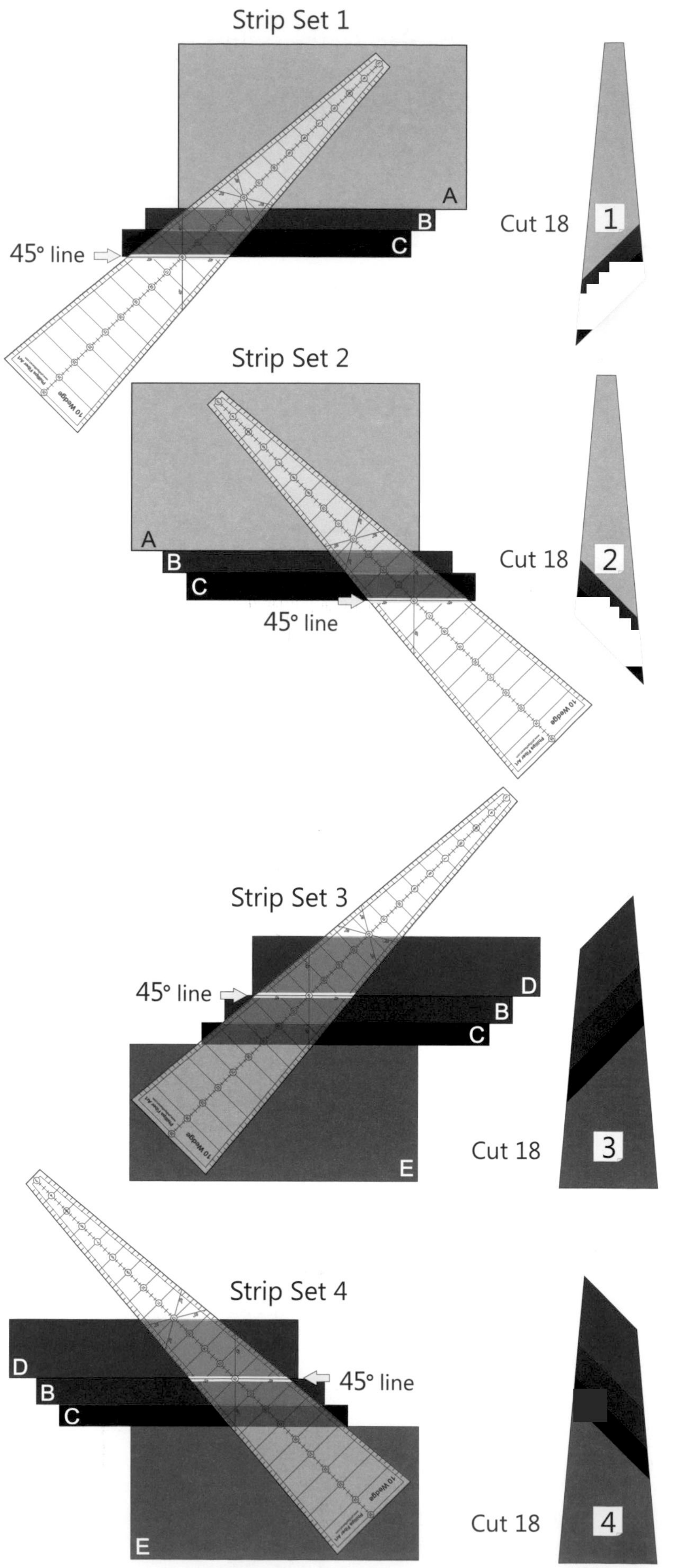

Marking Wedge Pieces 3-4

1. Place a wedge piece #3 on the cutting board with widest part toward you.
2. Rotate the wedge tool to the left (counterclockwise).
3. Align the 45 degree line to the side edge of the fabric wedge with the right side of the 17 inch line just touching the D/B seam.

   Note: This is a precise placement!
   The marked line should be consistent on all wedges.

4. Using a fine mechanical pencil (see page 5) draw a line on the right side of the fabric wedge. Mark ***eighteen*** #3 wedge pieces.

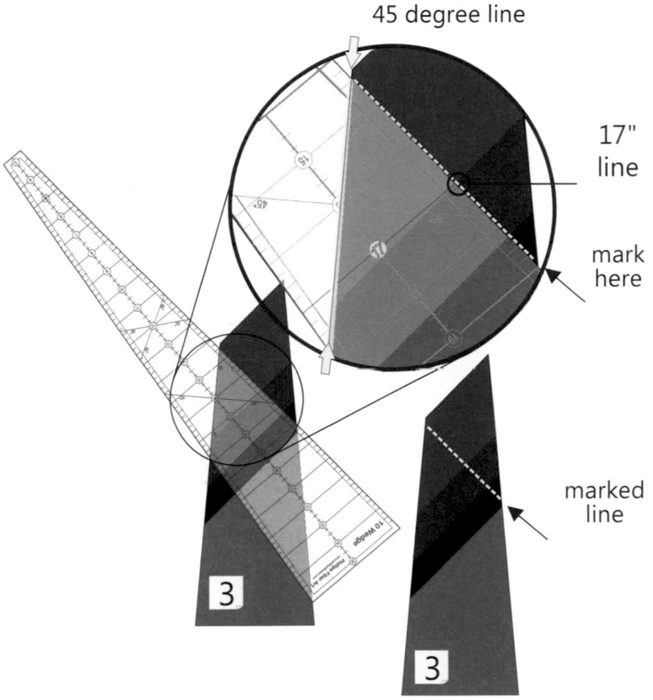

5. Repeat for the ***eighteen*** #4 wedge pieces, rotating the wedge tool to the right.

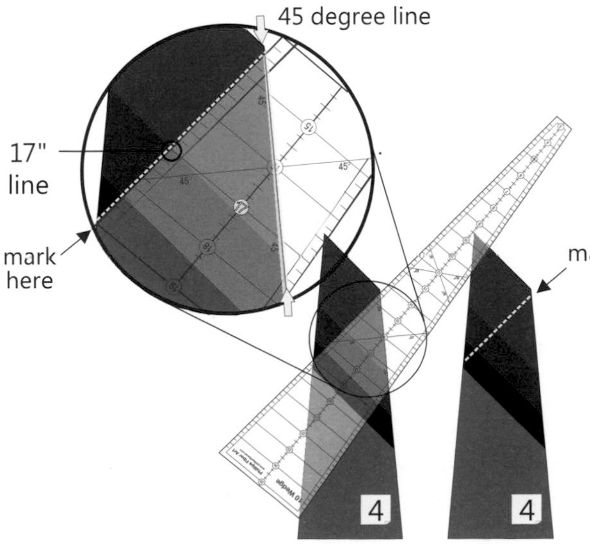

Sorting the Wedge Pieces

1. Group wedge pieces:

   #1 with #4 and
   #2 with #3 as shown.

Note:
The marked line is for placement, not stitching.

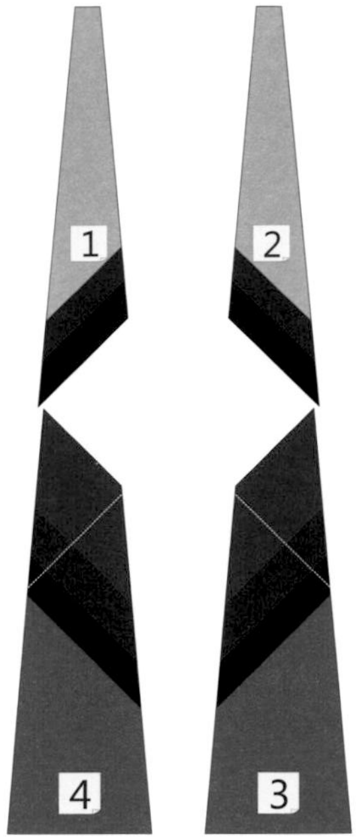

Assembling Wedges

1. Place wedge piece #2 onto the #3 wedge piece, aligning the edge with the marked line, allowing for the ¼" seam.
2. Sew the two pieces together ¼" from the marked edge.
3. Open and line up #2 with the underlying portion of #3 as indicated by arrow.

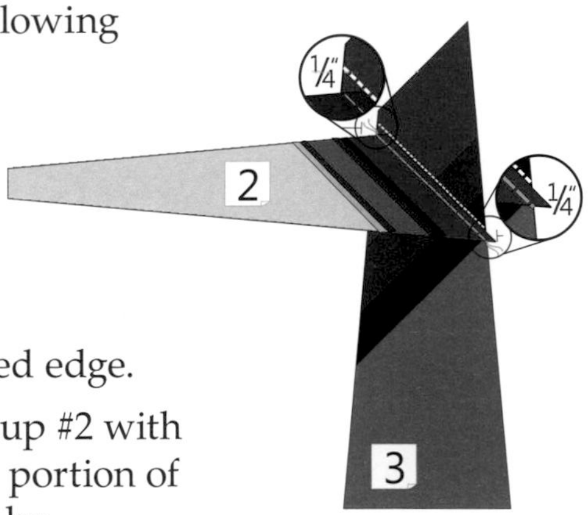

4. If they align, finger press the seam being careful not to distort the bias edges.

   If they do not align, remove the stitching, adjust and re-sew.

5. Trim away the excess #3 wedge piece. Label R.

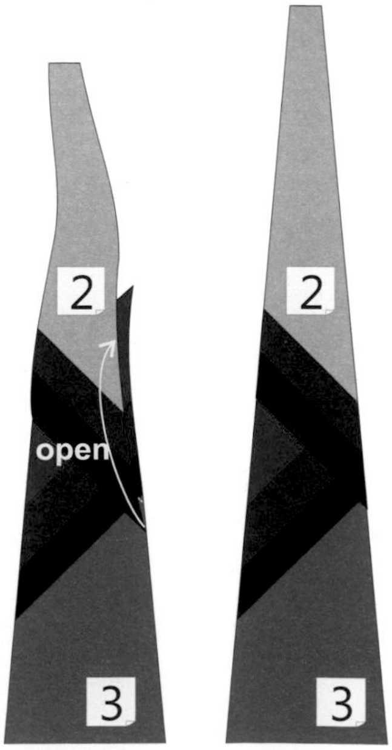

Assembling Wedges (Continued)

1. Place wedge piece #1 onto wedge piece #4, aligning the edge with the marked line, allowing for the ¼" seam.
2. Sew the two pieces together ¼" from the marked edge.

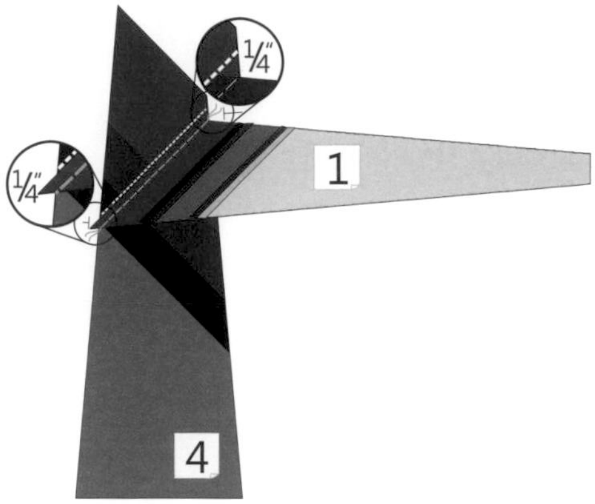

3. Open and line up #1 with the underlying portion of #4 indicated by arrow.
4. If they align, finger press the seam being careful not to distort the bias edges.
   If they do not align, remove the stitching, adjust, re-sew.

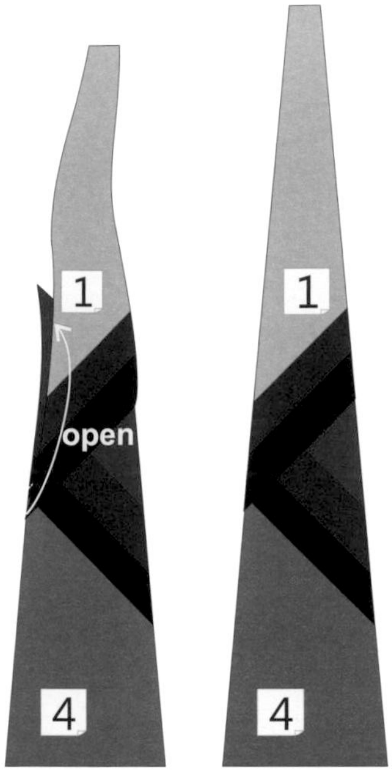

5. Trim away the excess #4 wedge piece. Label L.

Sewing Wedge Pairs

1. Place a R wedge onto a L wedge.
2. Pin each matching seam.
3. Sew the two wedges together with exact ¼" seams.

4. Sew the remaining wedges together in pairs. You will have ***eighteen*** wedge pairs.
5. Do not press at this point.

Sew 18 pairs

Step Three Constructing the Circle

1. Sew wedge pairs together until a circle is formed.
2. Press the seams following the instructions on page 54.

Center Applique

⌘ Trace a circle for the center applique, page 61.
⌘ Make the applique with Fabric A.
⌘ Applique the circle to the center of the quilt.

Step Four Finishing

The Chained Melody quilt top is now ready for the finishing process. You will find the help you need in the *Basic Instructions* on page 56.

Creative Options

These suggestions are only intended to inspire. You'll want to make the basic pattern before trying variations.

Playing with the Chain

Unchained Melody

Follow the same instructions as you would for a Chained Melody, but only make the left wedge.

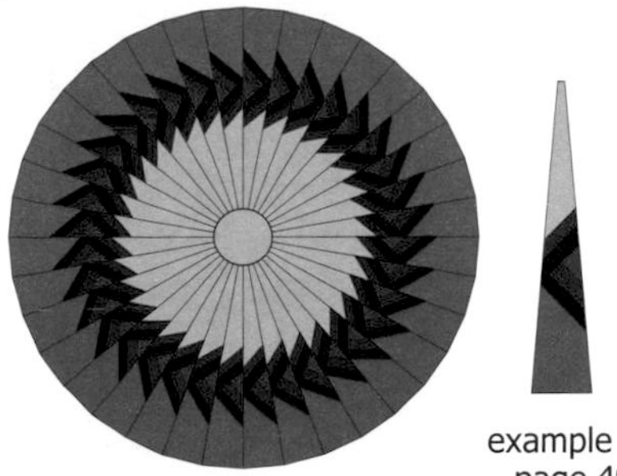

example on page 49

Playing with Color

Background Colors

Make left and right wedges using different A and E fabrics. Cut ***three each*** of A-1, A-2, E-1 and E-2 strips. Suggested yardage is ⅞ yard for each fabric.

example on page 35

Playing with Stripes

Vertical stripes

In the sample to the right, the stripe is cut vertically.

Chain colors

Cut three strips each of Fabrics B-1, B-2, D-1 and D-2. Reduce the yardage for the B and D fabrics to ⅜ yard each. Yardage for Fabrics A, C and E remains the same as the basic pattern.

Horizontal stripes

In the sample to the right, the stripe is cut horizontally.

Chain color shuffle

Rearrange the chain on the left and right sides.

Playing with Solid Wedges

Alternate a Chained Melody wedge pair with solid wedges.

Color A	Four Strips	8" x width	1 ¼ yd
Color B	Eight Strips	1 ½" x width	½ yd
Color C	Eight Strips	1 ½" x width	½ yd
Color D	Four Strips	3" x width	½ yd
Color E	Four Strips	6 ¾" x width	2 ⅛ yd
	Two Strips*	23" x width	

** may be possible with one strip*

Make ***twelve*** wedge pairs from two strip sets of each set, referring to the basic pattern for detailed instructions. Cut ***twelve*** solid wedges from the 23" Fabric E strips, and sew between each pair.

Just Play!

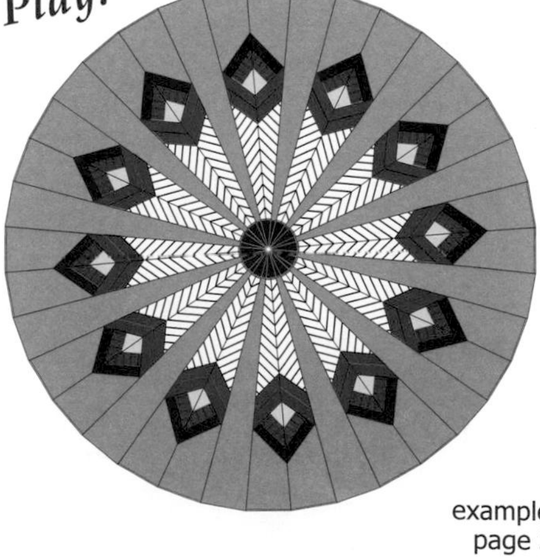

example on page 35

Playing with Border Stripes

To use a border stripe in place of the pieced strips, substitute single strips for Strips B, C and D.

Cut ***six*** 2 ½" wide strips for Strip Sets 1 and 2.
Cut ***six*** 5" wide strips for Strip Sets 3 and 4.

On the back side of the strip set, mark a line 2" from the E seam. Substitute this line for the D/B placement of the wedge tool. Cut the wedge pieces from the back side of the fabric.

Yardage varies with the number of repeats of the desired stripe. Always purchase more than you think you need for border stripes!

Changing Size

25" Chained Melody

Refer to the basic pattern for detailed instructions.

⌘ Use the Mini Ten Degree Wedge template for a 25" Chained Melody. Trace the 45 degree markings onto the template or tool following the lines found on page 61.

Cutting

Color A	Four Strips	4" x width	⅝ yd
Color B	Eight Strips	1" x width	⅓ yd
Color C	Eight Strips	1" x width	⅓ yd
Color D	Four Strips	2 ¼" x width	⅓ yd
Color E	Four Strips	3" x width	½ yd

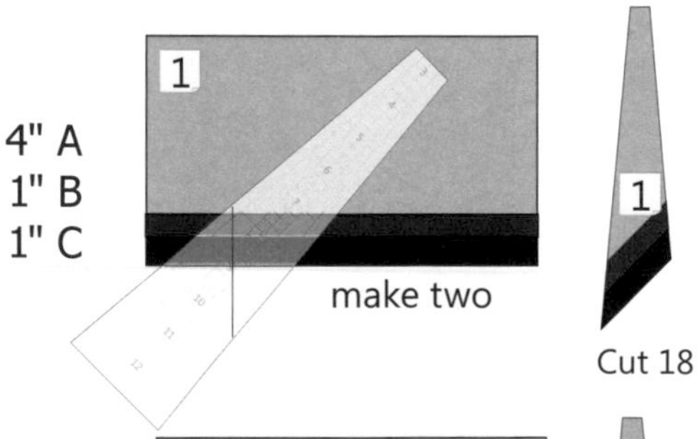

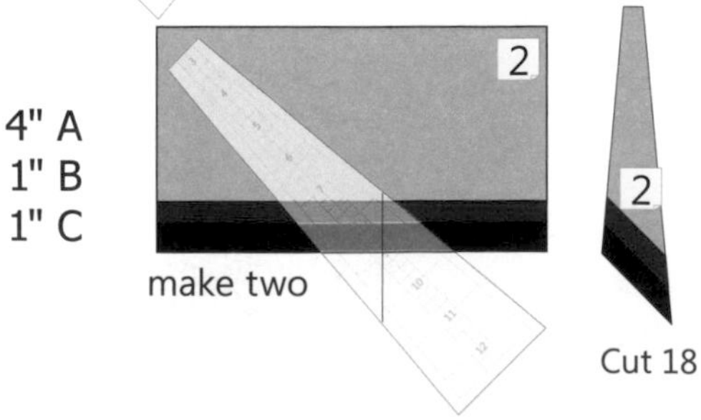

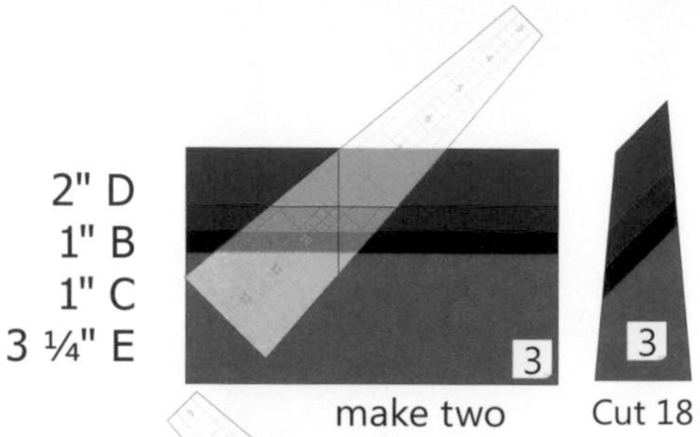

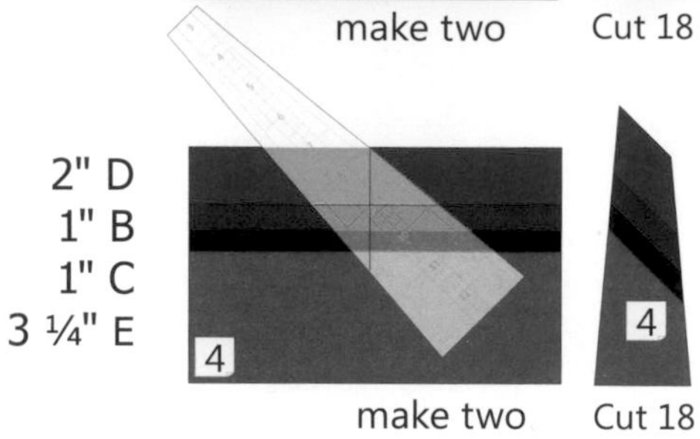

⌘ Place the traced 45 degree line of the Mini Wedge onto the side of the # 3 piece, aligning the 10" line to the D/B seam as shown.
Note the position of the wide end of the wedge tool.

⌘ Mark a line along the edge of the wedge.

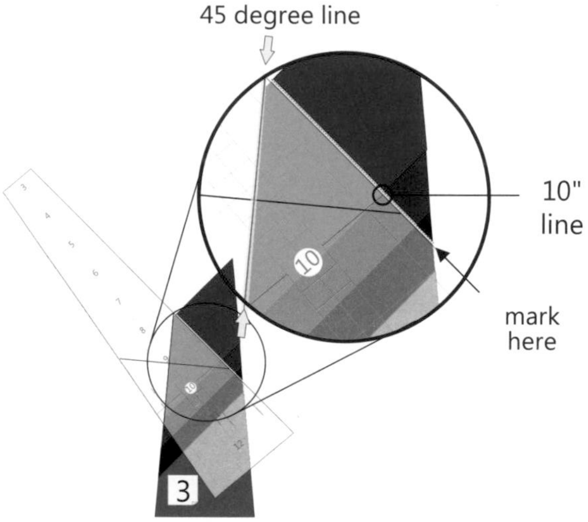

⌘ Repeat for the #4 piece, rotating the wedge tool.

⌘ Assemble following the pattern instructions.

⌘ Applique the center with the same sized circle used for the full version.

Variations with 25 inch Circles

Solid Wedge Variation

Refer to the instructions on the previous page.
Reduce the number of strips and yardage by half.
Cut ***one*** 10" strip of Fabric E for the solid wedges.

Border Stripe Variation

Refer to the instructions from the top of this page.
Cut ***four*** 1 ½" wide strips for Strip Sets 1 & 2 and ***four*** 2 ½" wide strips for Strip Sets 3 & 4.
On the back side of the 2 ½" strip, mark a line 1" from the E seam.

Jazzy Jolt
Page 36

Floating Diamonds
Jazzy Jolt Variation
Page 39

Chained Melody
Page 41

Jazzy Jolt
Page 36

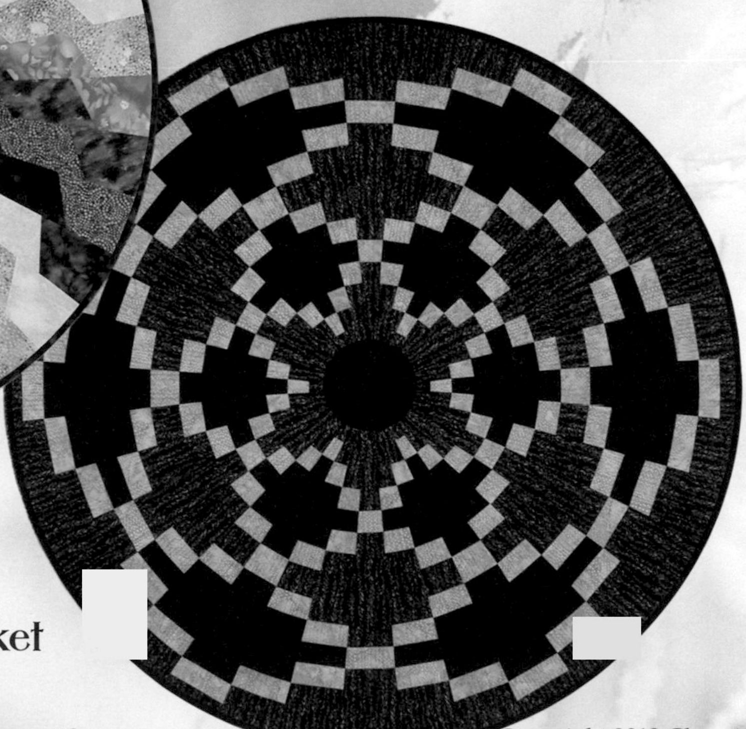

Woven Basket
Page 51

Jazzy Jolt
Page 36

Chained Melody Variation
Page 46

Just Play!

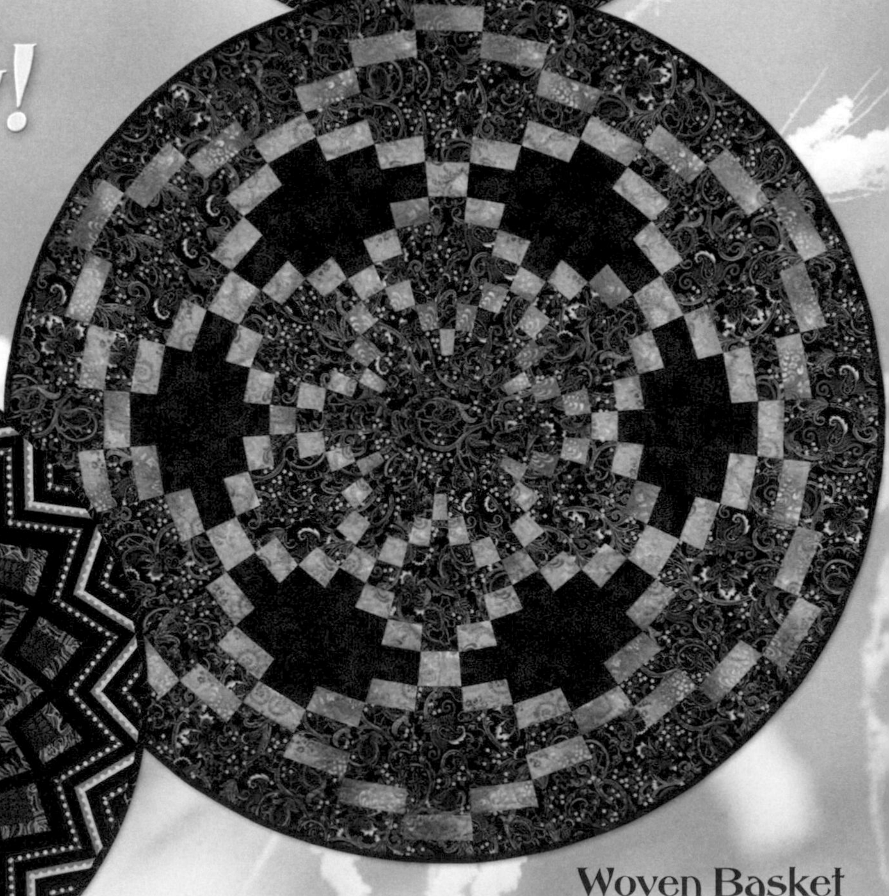

Woven Basket
Page 51

Chained Melody

Woven Basket

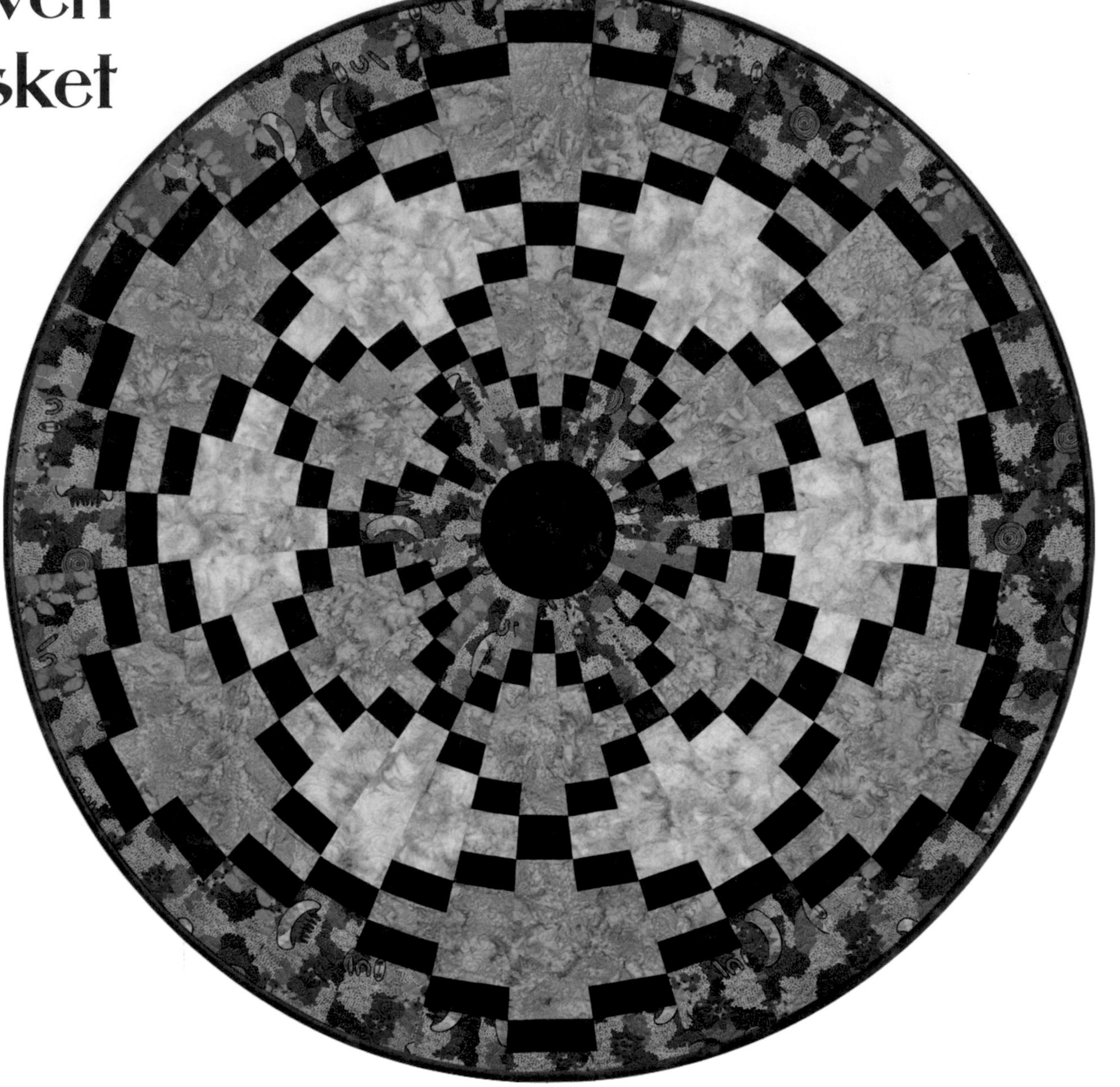

Be sure to read over both the introduction, pages 4 and 5, and the basic instructions, page 54 to 57 before beginning your project.

Finished Circle
50″ in diameter

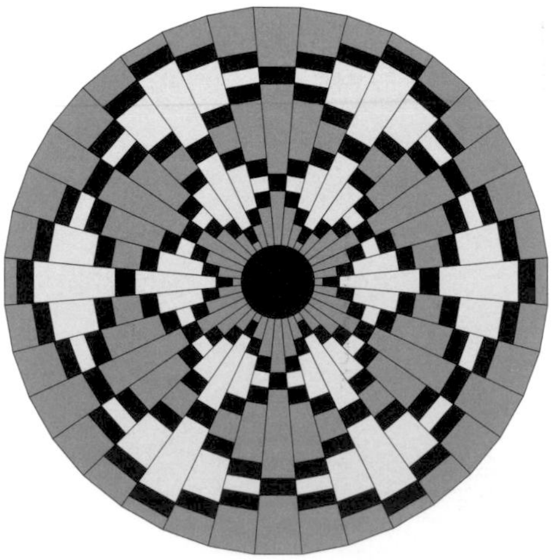

A

B

C

D

Fabric

Color A	1 1/8 yd	[34" actual]
Color B	1 1/8 yd	[34" actual]
Color C	3/4 yd	[17" actual]
Color D	1 yd	[30" actual]
Binding	1/2 yd	
Backing	3 yd	
Batting	54" x 54"	

For stripes parallel to the selvage, increase the yardage to 1 ¼ yd and cut along the lengthwise grain.

Cutting

Cut strips in the widths as shown below. Group and label the strips according to width and color.

Color A

Two Strips	6 1/2" x 22 1/2"
Two Strips	5" x width
Two Strips	3 1/2" x width
Two Strips	2" x 22 1/2"

Color B

One Strip	2 1/2" x 22 1/2"
Four Strips	2" x 22 1/2"
Eight Strips	2" x width
One Square	7" x 7"

Color C

One Strip	8 1/2" x 22 1/2"
One Strip	5 1/2" x width
One Strip	2 1/2" x width

Color D

Two Strips	8" x 22 1/2"
Two Strips	5" x width
Two Strips	2" x width

Step One   Sewing the Strip Sets

- *Sew **exact** ¼" seams through out.*
- *Label all strip sets as shown.*

Strip Sets 1-4

1. Sew Strip Set 1 in the order shown.
2. Repeat for Strip Sets 2-4 as shown.

Press all seam allowances toward the center of the B strips.

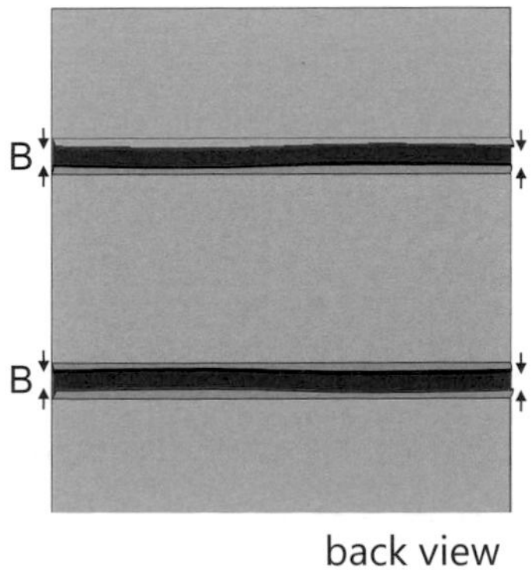

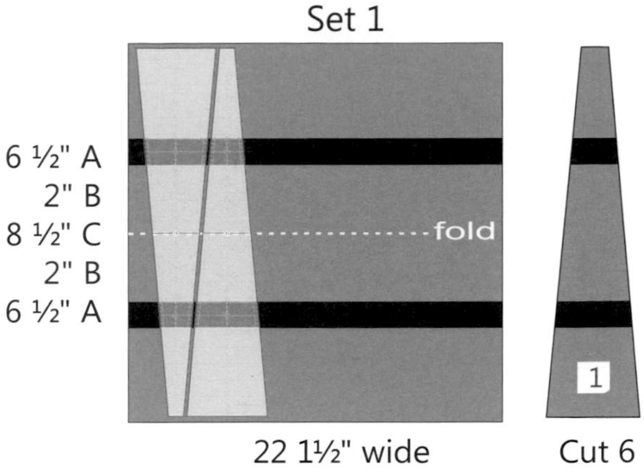

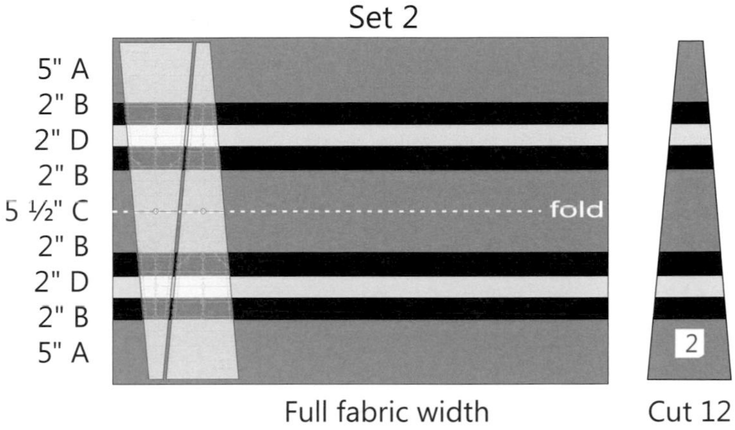

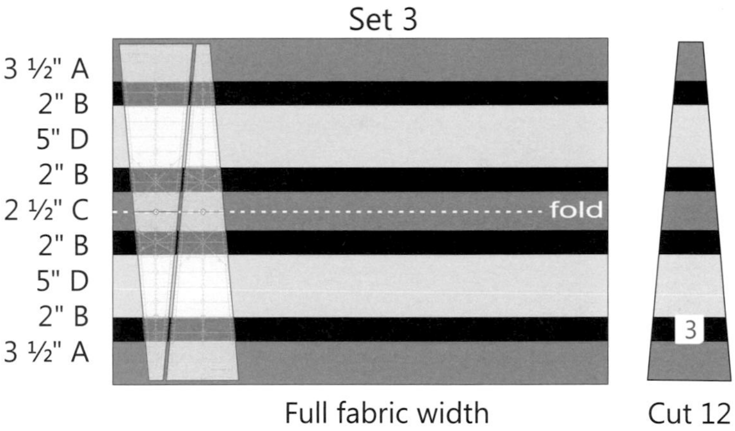

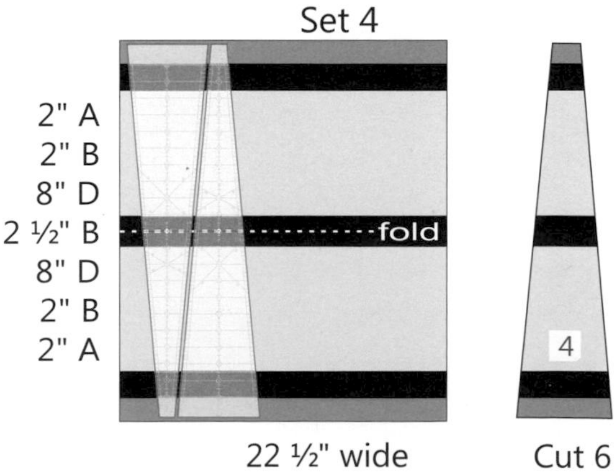

Step Two Cutting the Wedges

Prepare the wedge tool with non-slip adhesive rings or loops of tape. See page 54.

Strip Sets 1-4

- Fold each strip set in half lengthwise.
- Press the fold lightly to crease, then unfold the strip set.
- Rotate the wedge tool for each cut, cutting close to the previous cut to assure having enough fabric.

1. Place the 14" line of the wedge tool on the folded crease of Strip Set 1.
   Cut ***six*** identical wedges. Label as 1.

2. Place the 14" line of the wedge tool on the folded crease of Strip Set 2.
   Cut ***twelve*** identical wedges. Label as 2.

3. Place the 14" line of the wedge tool on the folded crease of Strip Set 3.
   Cut ***twelve*** identical wedges. Label as 3.

4. Place the 14" line of the wedge tool on the folded crease of Strip Set 4.
   Cut ***six*** identical wedges. Label as 4.

Step Three Constructing the Circle

Sewing Wedges

1. Layout wedges in order.
2. Match the seams and pin.
3. Sew wedges together to make the circle.
4. Press after the top is complete.

Find tips on Pressing on page 55.

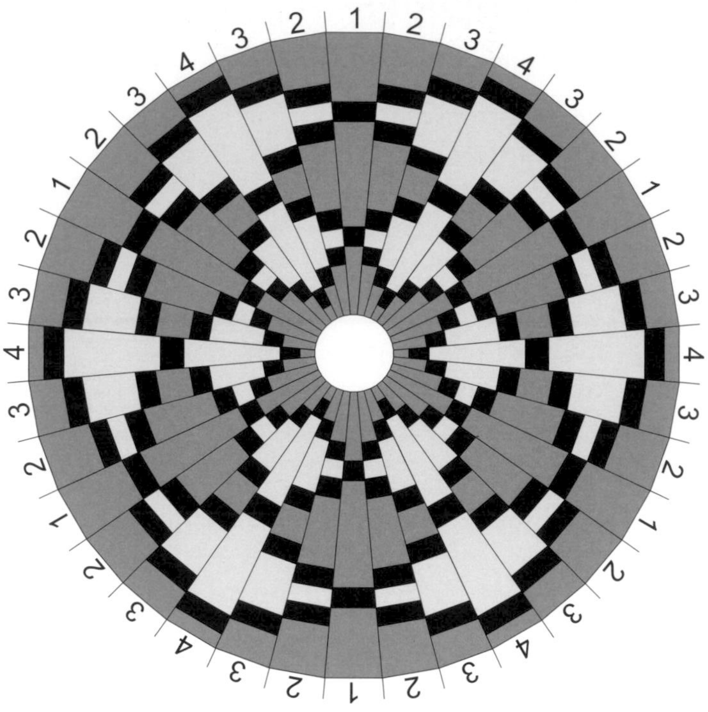

Center Applique

- Trace the circle from page 61 for your center applique.
- Make the applique using the 7" Fabric B square. See page 54 for complete applique instructions.
- Applique the circle to the center of the quilt.

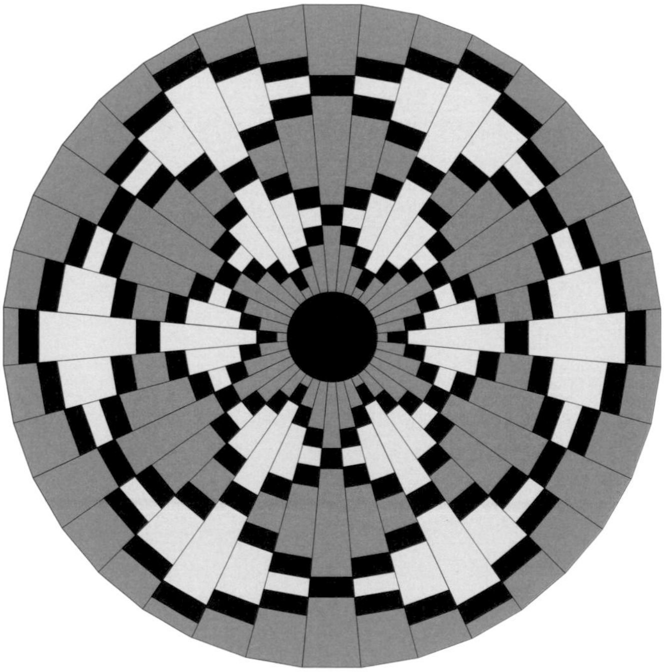

Step Four Finishing

The Basket quilt top is now ready for the finishing process. You will find the help you need in the *Basic Instructions* on page 56.

Basic Instructions

Cutting Strips

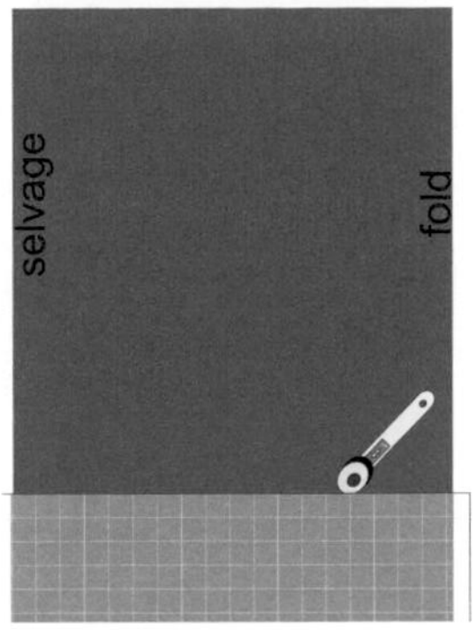

Press fabric with spray starch before cutting to add stability to both strips and wedges. This is helpful when handling bias edges.

Cut strips across the full fabric width. Strip width must be accurate.

- Measure with your acrylic ruler, not the cutting mat. The measuring grid on most cutting mats will not provide the accuracy you need to ensure successful results.

For strips wider than your ruler, measure and mark the proper strip width as follows:

- Measure from the edge of the strip and mark the same measurement in three places, the middle, and both ends of the strip.
- Align the marks with your straight-edge and cut.

Cutting Wedges

All wedges must be cut ***exactly*** the same size and shape as your wedge tool.

Important: *to prevent slippage, apply a non-slip adhesive product or several long tubes of wide transparent tape, sticky side out, to the back of the wedge tool.*

- Place your wedge tool on the strip set as shown in the illustrations.

For the most ergonomic cutting position, place the strip sets perpendicular to your body and the wedge tool parallel to your body. As you make each cut, shift your body from side to side.

When cutting the wedge vertical to your body, your wrist will be fully extended at the end of the wedge, making it difficult to cut accurately.

- Follow placement diagrams exactly.
- Cut the long sides first, then along the wide and narrow ends of the wedge tool.
- To conserve fabric, reposition the wedge tool so it touches the previous cut.

Straight-cut Wedges

Place the correct inch markings of your wedge tool on the seams indicated in the pattern illustrations.

The strip set seams must be parallel to the inch lines on the wedge tool. Adjust the fabric so seams are aligned. Precision at this stage will ensure the design lines match when sewing them together.

Angle-cut Wedges

For the Chained Melody pattern, both portions of the wedge are cut following the 45 degree line found on the wedge tool.

For the Jazzy Jolt pattern, additional 60 degree lines are marked on the wedge tool.

- Refer to the pattern illustrations for precise placement on the seam lines.

Labeling

Labeling is the key to organization. Create your own labels following the specific suggestions in each pattern or download label pages from the www.phillipsfiberart.com web site. Pin or tape an identifying label to the following items:

- **Strips**: Label the strips by letter and width as given in the cutting instructions for each pattern.
- **Strip Sets**: Label the strip sets as shown in the illustrations.
- **Wedges**: Label the wedges as shown in the illustrations.

Pinning Wedges

When sewing individual or groups of wedges together, pin carefully as follows:

- Place the wedges on a flat surface to pin.

This is especially important for angle-cut wedges.

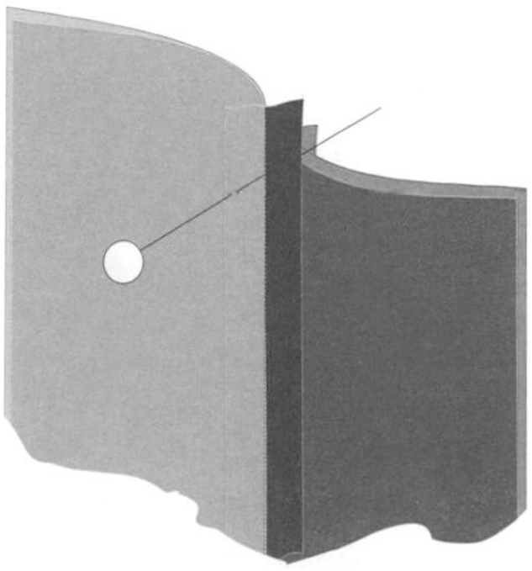

Pin precisely at the matching points, using your pin to align the seams and at both ends of the fabric wedges as they have a tendency to stretch.

Seam Allowance

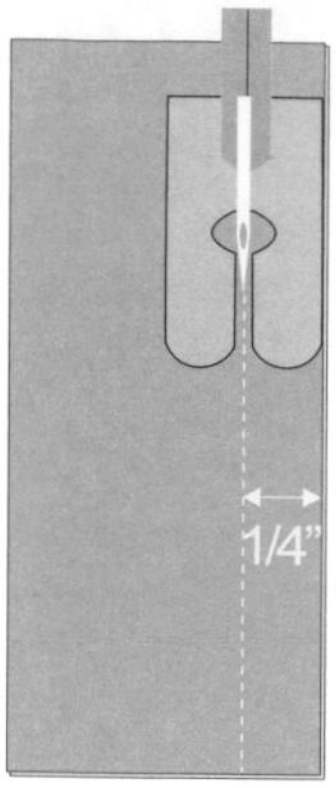

- Use ***exact*** 1/4" seams throughout. A 1/4" presser foot is extremely helpful.
- Consistent seam allowances are crucial to your success.

Offsetting Strips

For the Jazzy Jolt or Chained Melody patterns offset the strips in a stair stepping fashion for the best use of fabric.

Sewing Strip Sets

- Shorten the stitch length on your sewing machine to keep stitches from coming apart when the wedges are cut from the strip sets.
- Sew the strip sets following the order shown in the various pattern illustrations. Use care to choose the correct size fabric strip for each strip set.

Sewing Wedges

- Sewing the wedges together from the narrow end to the wide end is recommended.
- The wedges are the same size. Match and pin at both the wide and narrow ends.
- To lock the stitching, back stitch at both the beginning and end of the wedge seam.

Be aware, the narrow end of the wedge has a tendency to float away from a true ¼" seam allowance.

Pressing

- Press fabric with spray starch before cutting to add stability to both strips and wedges. This is helpful when handling bias edges.
- Careful pressing is crucial to the success of making a circle quilt. Press seams from the back and then the front avoiding any pleats along the seam lines.

Avoid pulling or stretching the fabric out of shape.

Pressing Strip Sets

- Place the strip set to be pressed, wrong side up, on the ironing board with the seams parallel to the length of the ironing surface.
- Press the seam allowances as indicated in each pattern. Make the seams straight and parallel to each other. Turn the strip set over, right-side-up, and press again firmly.

Pressing Circles

Press only when the wedges are sewn into a complete circle. Pressing before the circle is completed leads to distortion. It is especially easy to stretch the center opening.

Trace a circle from page 61 with a permanent marker onto muslin and place on the ironing surface. Place your circle quilt, right side down, with the opening centered to the drawn circle. Shift the center until it forms a symmetrical circular opening.

- Gently press the opening, pressing the seam allowances in a counter-clockwise direction.

Stabilize the center opening with an 8 inch square of freezer paper, waxy side down before moving the quilt on the ironing surface.

- Press the circle from the back before pressing the front side. Press lightly with the seam allowances going counter-clockwise to make appliqueing the center easier.
- Press from the front being careful to maintain the circular shape of both the entire piece as well as the center opening.

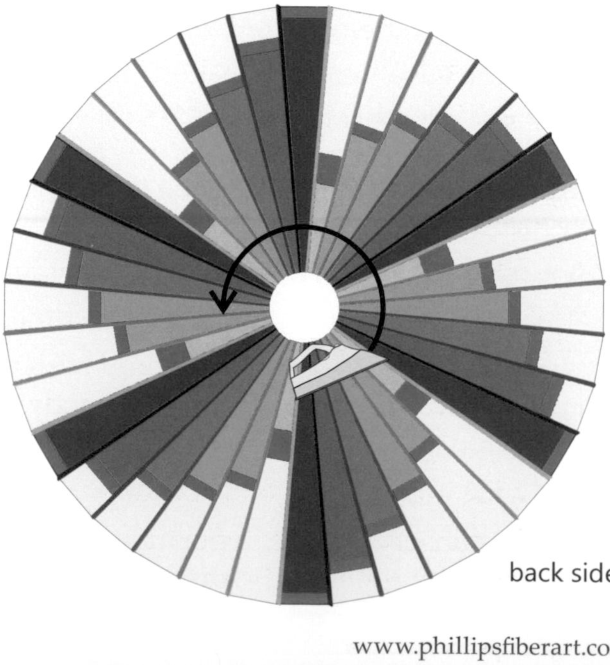

back side

Center Appliques

Freezer Paper Method

1. Stabilize the center opening by ironing a ***eight*** inch square of freezer paper, waxy side down to the wrong side of the quilt top center.
2. Measure the diameter of the center opening. If it is larger than 5 ⅝" enlarge the template circle.
3. Trace the circle template pattern from page 61 onto the dull side of another piece of freezer paper.
4. Cut out the freezer paper pattern. Iron the waxy side to the wrong side of the center appliqué fabric.
5. Cut the applique fabric ¼" larger than the paper.
6. Using a fabric basting glue stick, apply glue to the edge of the paper.
7. Turn the extending fabric over and finger press down to the glued edge of the paper.
8. Place the appliqué over the center opening of the circle quilt and pin in place.
9. Appliqué by hand or machine.
10. Remove the paper from the fabric.

Fusible Interfacing Method

1. Stabilize the center opening with an 8 inch circle of fusible interfacing placed on the wrong side of the quilt top. Press only along the outer edge to avoid fusing the center to the ironing surface while maintaining the exact circle shape of the opening.
2. Measure the diameter of the center opening.
3. Trace the circle template pattern from page 61 onto the nonadhesive side of the fusible interfacing.
4. Place the adhesive side against the right side of the center appliqué fabric.
5. Stitch on the traced line.
6. Trim the two layers ¼" from the stitching.
7. Slit the interfacing with an "X" and turn the appliqué inside out.
8. Place the appliqué over the center opening and fuse in place. The two fusible layers will add to the stability of the project.
9. Appliqué by hand or machine.

Piecing Center Appliques

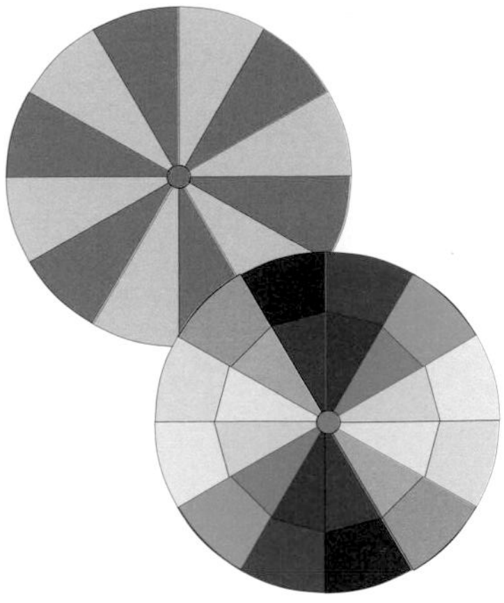

1. Trace the Mini 30 Degree Wedge found on page 61 onto template plastic.
2. Cut ***twelve*** wedges from selected fabrics or pieced sections as described in the individual pattern.
3. Sew the wedges together to form a circle.
4. Make a mini circle appliqué from page 61 using the freezer paper or fusible interfacing method.
5. Appliqué the mini circle over the center of the pieced circle.
6. Following the steps in ***Center Appliqués,*** left, create a center appliqué from the pieced circle.

Finishing

Backing

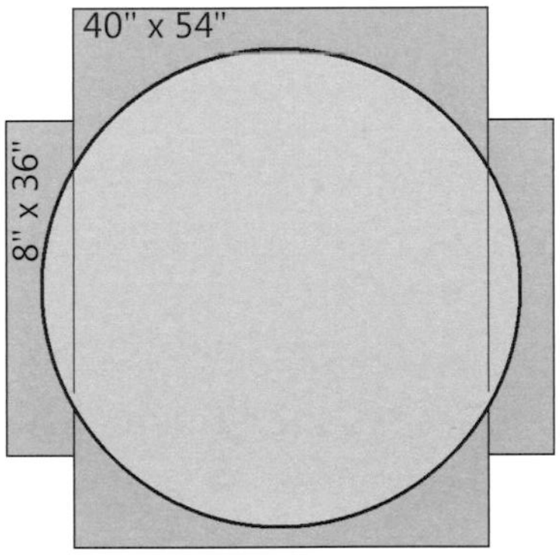

A 54" square is needed for backing the circular quilts. Piecing will be necessary if standard 40" fabric is used.

1. Trim the selvages from the 3 yard piece of 40"/44" wide backing fabric.
2. Cut a piece 54" x fabric width from the trimmed backing fabric. Set aside.
3. Cut two strips 8" x 36" from remaining fabric.
4. Center the 8" x 36" strips to the 54" sides of the large piece of backing. Sew the backing together.
5. Set aside the remaining piece of fabric for the sleeve.

Quilting

The quilts can be quilted by machine or hand. Simply outlining the piecing will give satisfactory results. With a little thought and imagination, however, you can greatly enhance the finished product.

Binding Circles

- After the circle quilt is quilted, measure the diameter.
- Cut 2 ½" wide bias strips from the 1/2 yard of binding fabric.

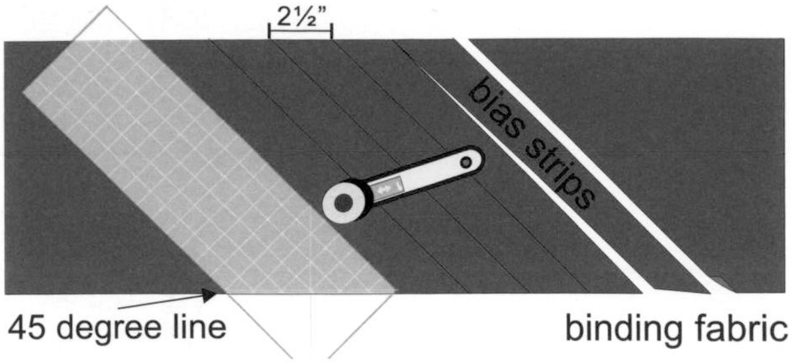

24"- 26" circles.............cut three strips
41"- 43" circles..................cut six strips
47"- 51" circles............cut seven strips
59"- 61" circles.............cut eight strips
69"- 71" circles...............cut nine strips

- Sew the bias strips together into one long strip as shown.
- Fold the bias strip in half and press, being careful not to stretch.
- Select the length needed for your circle.

Circle	Length	Circle	Diameter
24"	76"	50"	157 ¾"
25"	79 ¼"	51"	161"
26"	82"	59"	186"
41"	129 ½"	60"	189"
42"	132 ½"	61"	192 ¼"
43"	135 ½"	68"	214"
47"	148"	69"	217 ¼"
48"	151 ½"	70"	220 ½"
49"	154 ½"	71"	223 ½"

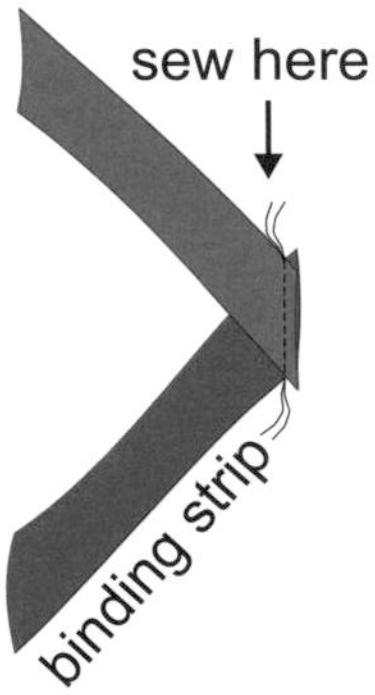

- Measure the binding strip along the fold for the length needed. Open the strip and cut at a parallel 45 degree angle.

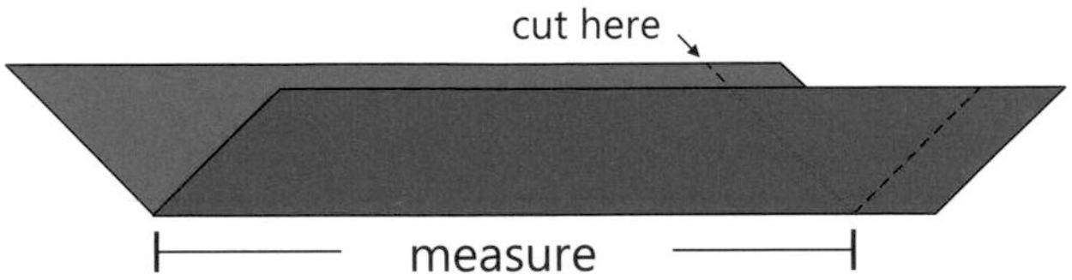

- Sew the ends of the strip together into a loop. Fold the loop into quarters and pin to mark.

The loop is the exact circumference of the quilted circle, avoiding stretching either the binding or edge of the quilt.

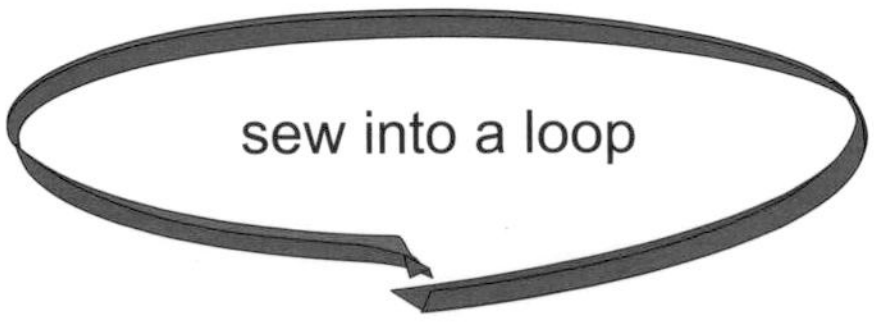

- Match the quarter marks of the binding and circle quilt. *Nine wedges equal one quarter.* Pin with right sides together evenly distributing any fullness.
- Sew the binding to the quilt with a ¼" seam.
- Fold to the back and hand stitch in place.

*For the **Speedy Spiral Tree Skirt**, cut three 2 ½" bias strips from fabric 13 ½" wide, by half the fabric width. Sew the three strips together and bind the sides and center opening.*

Hanging Your Circle Quilt

One method to successfully hang a circle quilt is adding a sleeve to the back of the quilted piece.

- Measure the diameter of the quilted circle. For the sleeve, cut 6" wide strip(s) of backing fabric by the diameter of the quilt.
- Sew a 2" hem on both ends of the strip.
- Fold the strip in half and sew into a tube and turn inside out.
- Hand sew the pocket to the quilted circle.
- Sew on three drapery rings.
- Cut a thin flat board to fit into the sleeve. Secure the board to the wall with small nails.
- Hang to the wall with pins placed in the drapery rings.

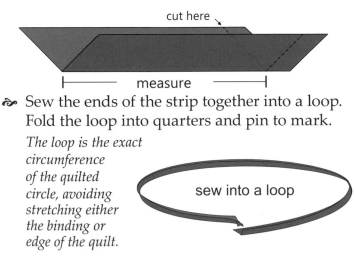

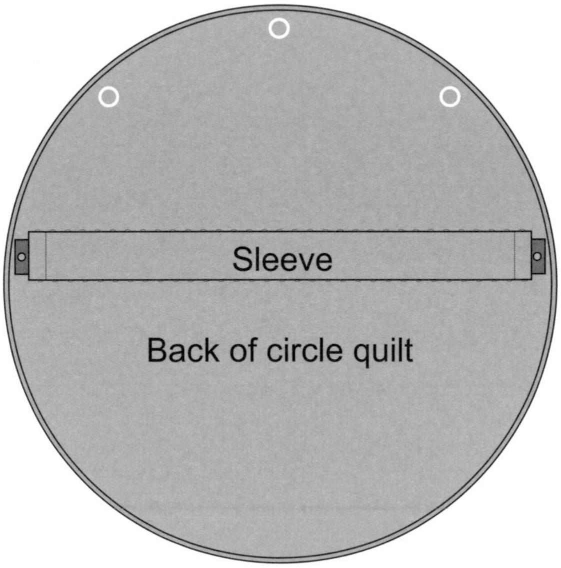

Use those dull sewing machine needles! They are stronger and leave a smaller hole in the wall. You can even nail them with a hammer. Enjoy!

A number of enterprising companies have created products for hanging quilts on the wall. Find a list of current companies and resources on the FAQ page on our web site: www.phillipsfiberart.com.

Framing Your Circle

1. Measure the diameter of your finished circle.
2. Photocopy the Framing Template pieces from pages 58 and 60. If copying, be sure to check the size to the book to be sure the photocopy machine did not alter the size. The template pieces can also be traced if preferred.
3. Tape the elements together carefully as shown.
4. Cut the template unit out choosing the appropriate line for your circle diameter measurement.

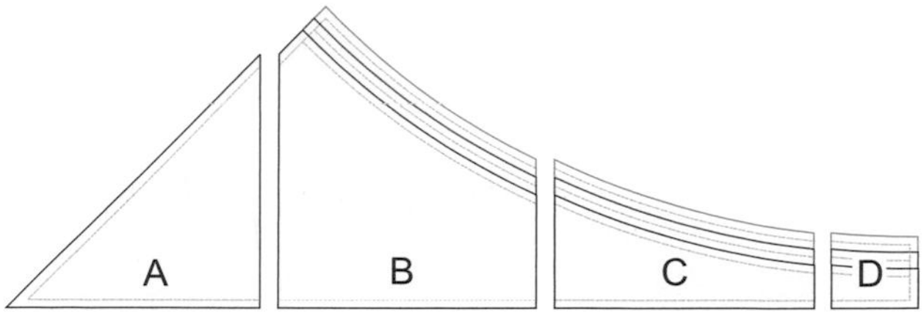

Tape the template pieces together to make the framing template. The lower edge of the template is 26 ⅝".

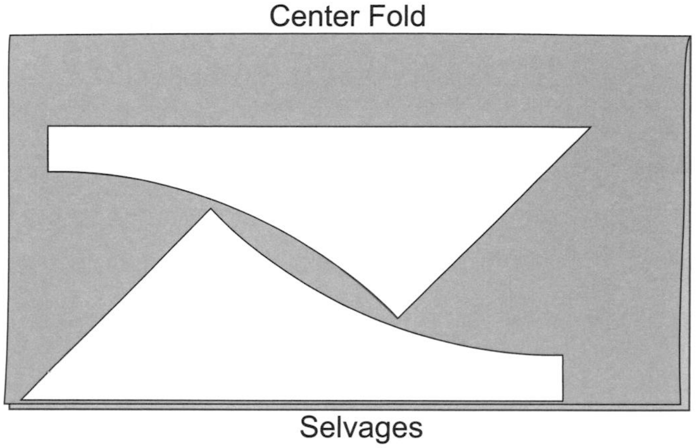

Making the Frame

1. The frame requires 1 ⅝ yard of non-directional fabric. Increase the yardage for stripes or other directional fabric, or fabric requiring selective cutting.
2. Either leave the framing fabric folded or place fabric pieces wrong sides together. Cutting two layers at once gives mirror images of the template piece. Cut ***eight*** framing pieces.
3. Sew the frame pieces together.

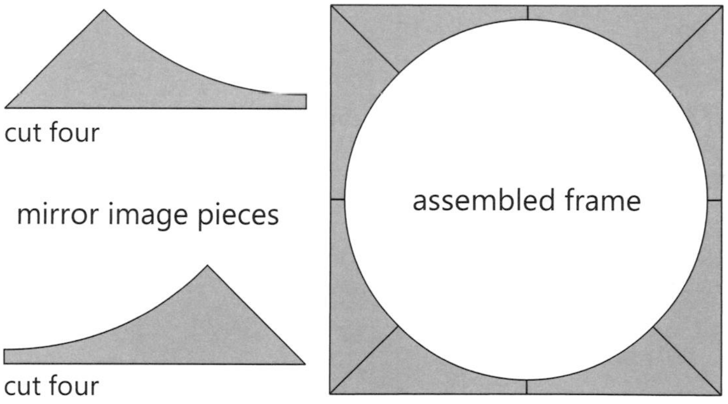

Assembling the Square

1. On a large flat surface, lay out your circle quilt right side up.
2. Place the assembled frame, right side up, on top of the circle. Position the frame to the circle to achieve the placement desired.
3. Bring the inner edge of the frame to the outside edge of the circle with right sides together.
4. Pin the frame to the pieced circle, evenly distributing frame to circle.
5. Sew the frame piece to the circle with a ¼" seam, keeping the circle section flat against the bed of the machine and the frame section on top to make a 52 inch square.

Continue to add borders or other elements to make the quilt the size desired.

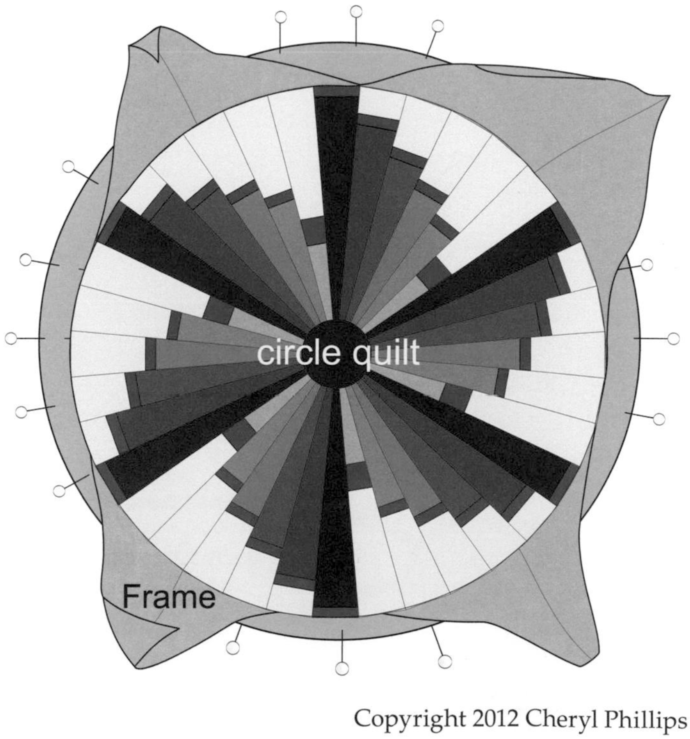

Photocopy or trace the four framing template pieces.
Tape together to form the template.
If copying, be sure to check the size to the book to be sure the photocopy machine did not alter the size.

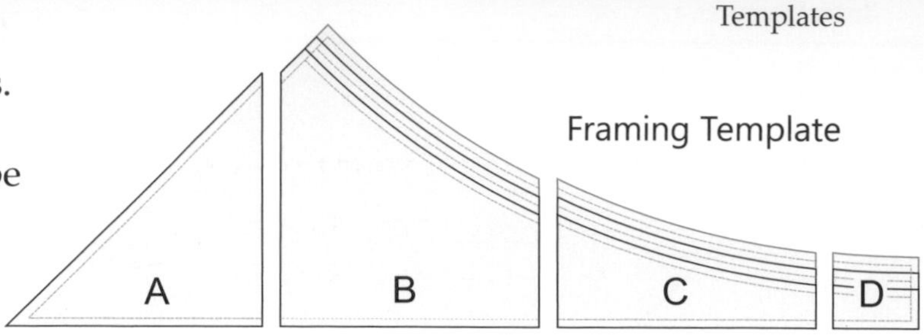

If your circle measures:
48" use the **blue line**
49" use the **red line**
50" use the **black line**

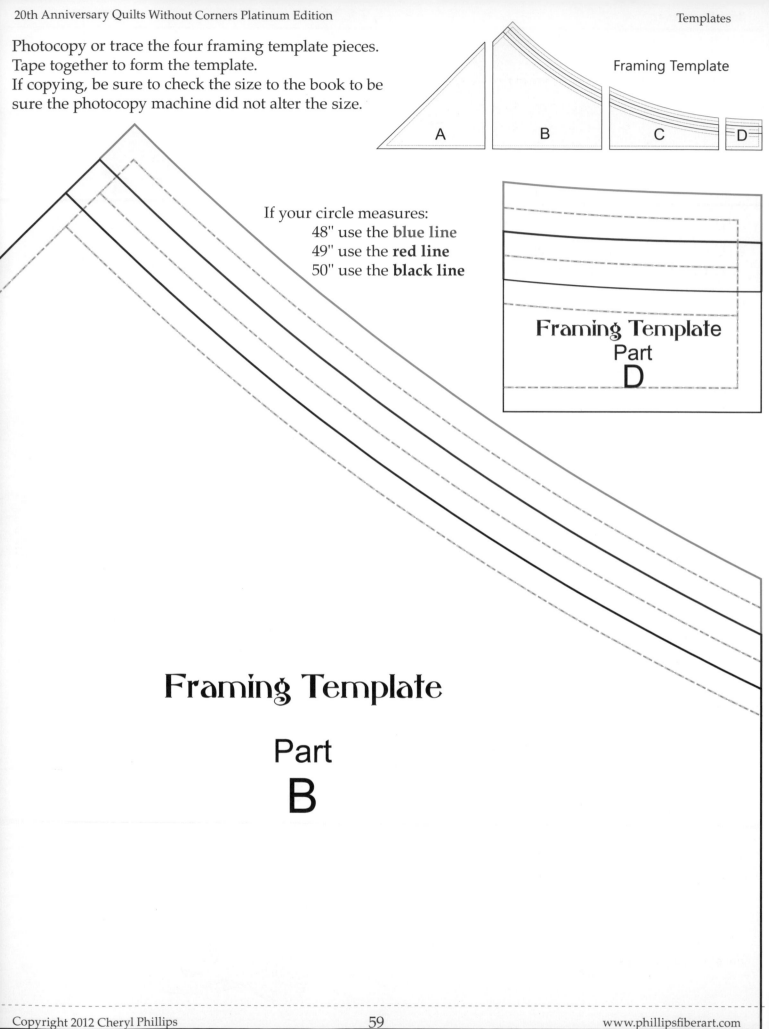

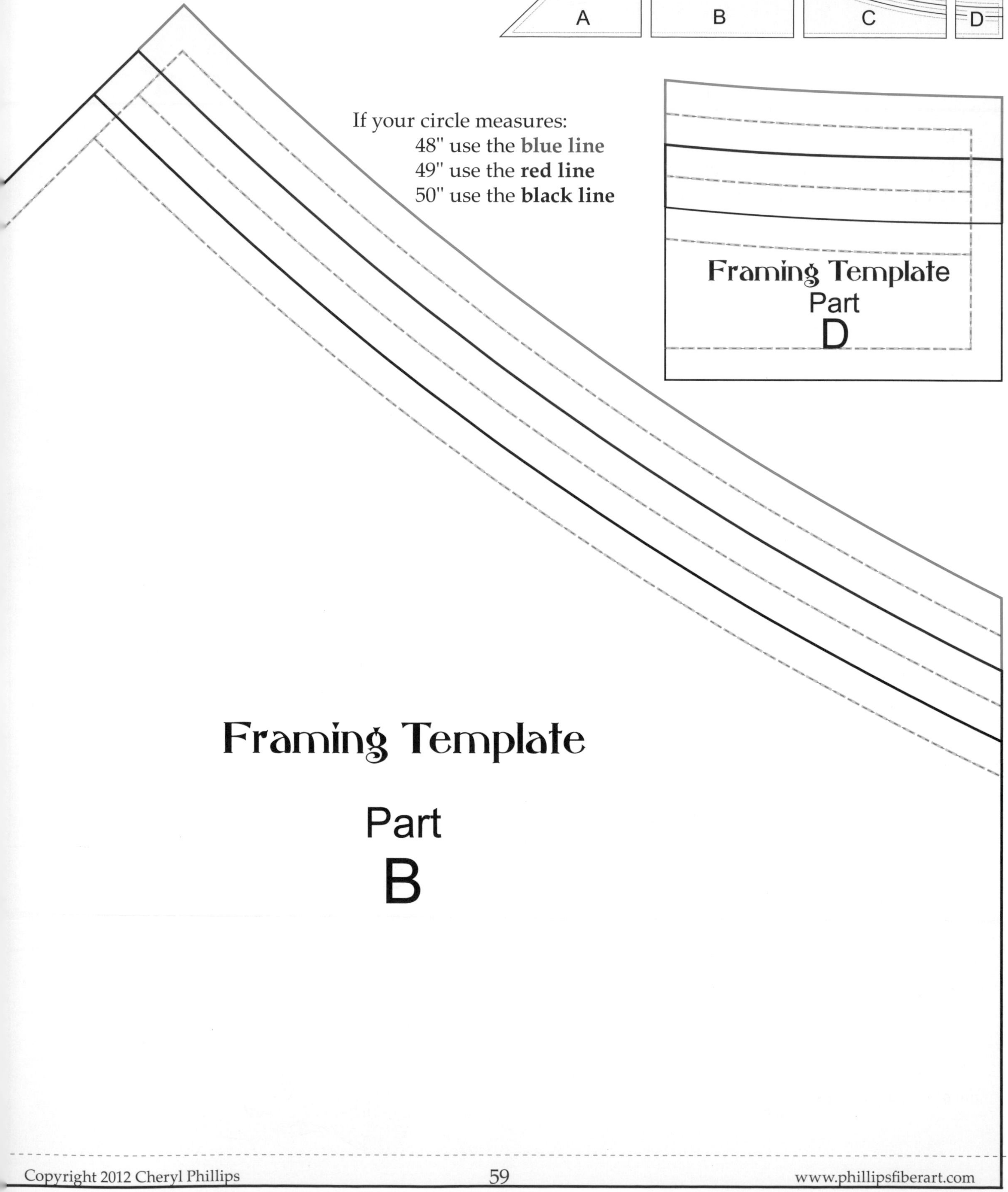

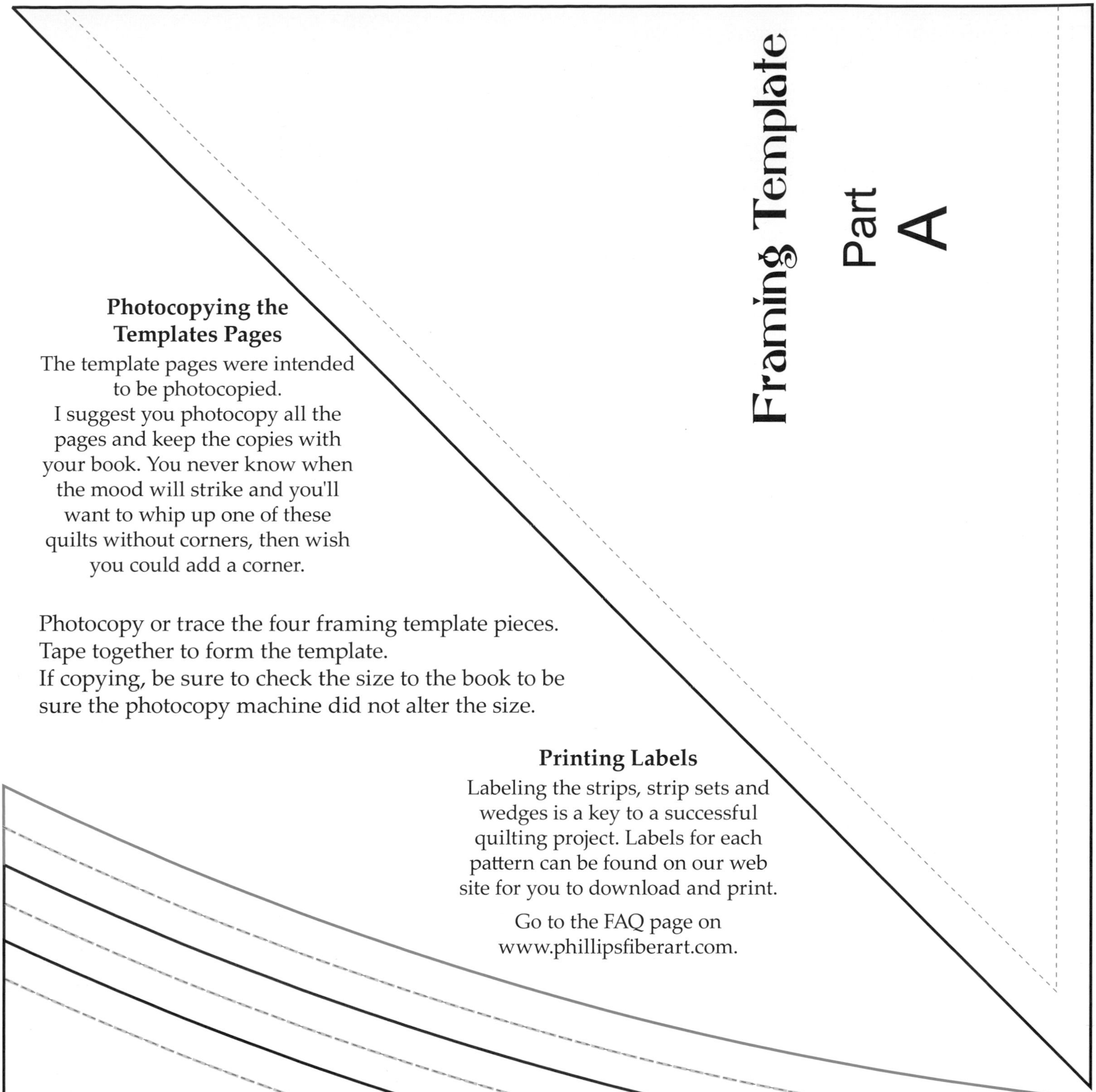

Photocopying the Templates Pages

The template pages were intended to be photocopied.
I suggest you photocopy all the pages and keep the copies with your book. You never know when the mood will strike and you'll want to whip up one of these quilts without corners, then wish you could add a corner.

Photocopy or trace the four framing template pieces.
Tape together to form the template.
If copying, be sure to check the size to the book to be sure the photocopy machine did not alter the size.

Printing Labels

Labeling the strips, strip sets and wedges is a key to a successful quilting project. Labels for each pattern can be found on our web site for you to download and print.

Go to the FAQ page on www.phillipsfiberart.com.

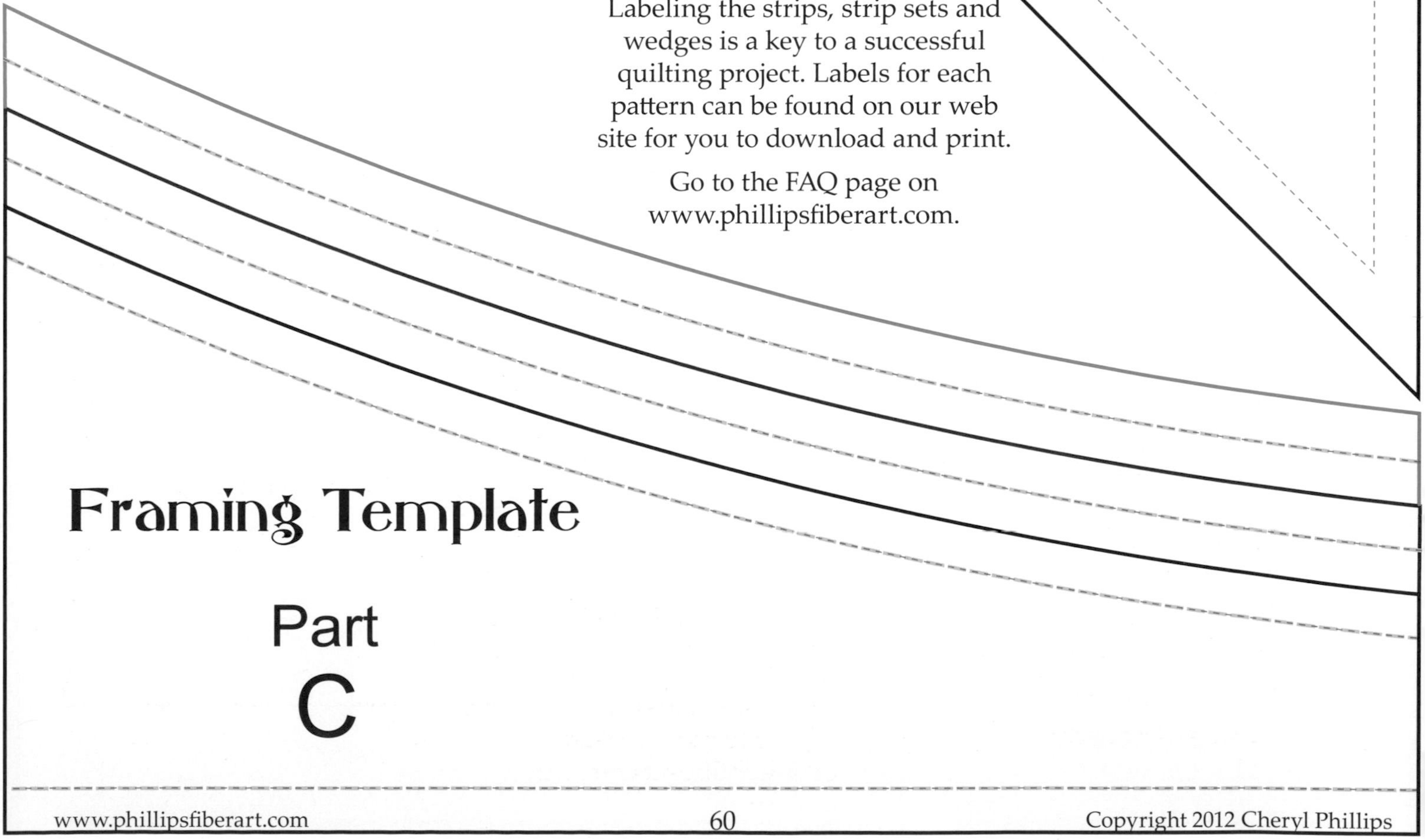

Refer to page 56 for instructions for making a freezer paper or fusible interfacing appliqué.

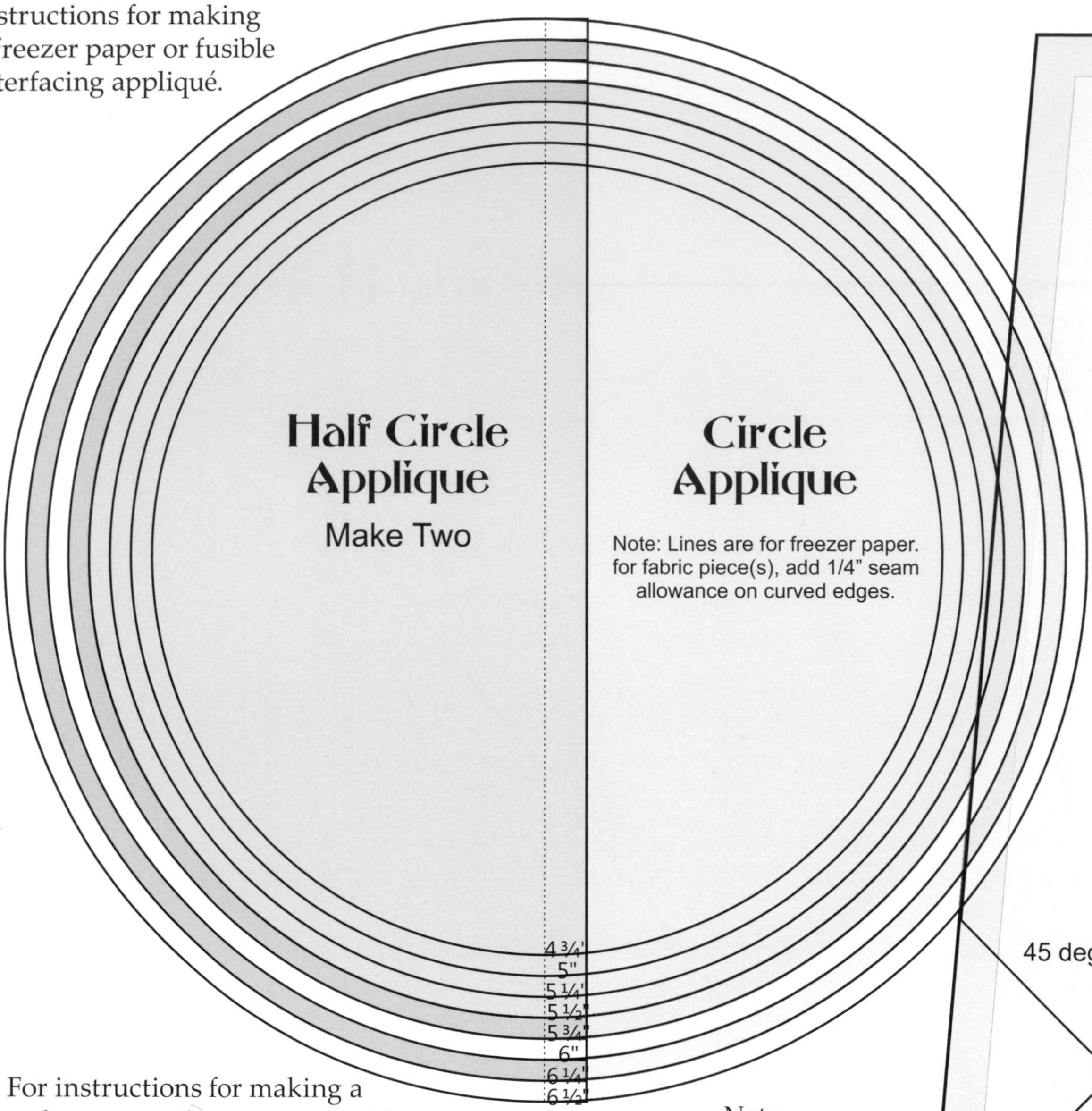

For instructions for making a pieced center applique, see page 56.

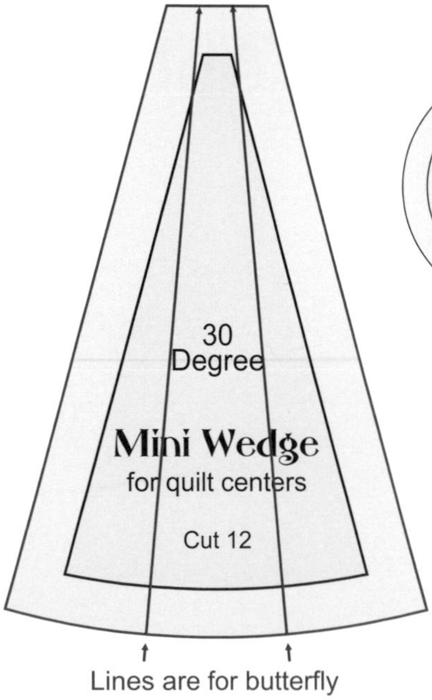

Note:
For a miniature Chained Melody, trace the 45 degree markings shown here onto your acrylic Mini Ten Degree Wedge, rather than the markings printed on the tool.

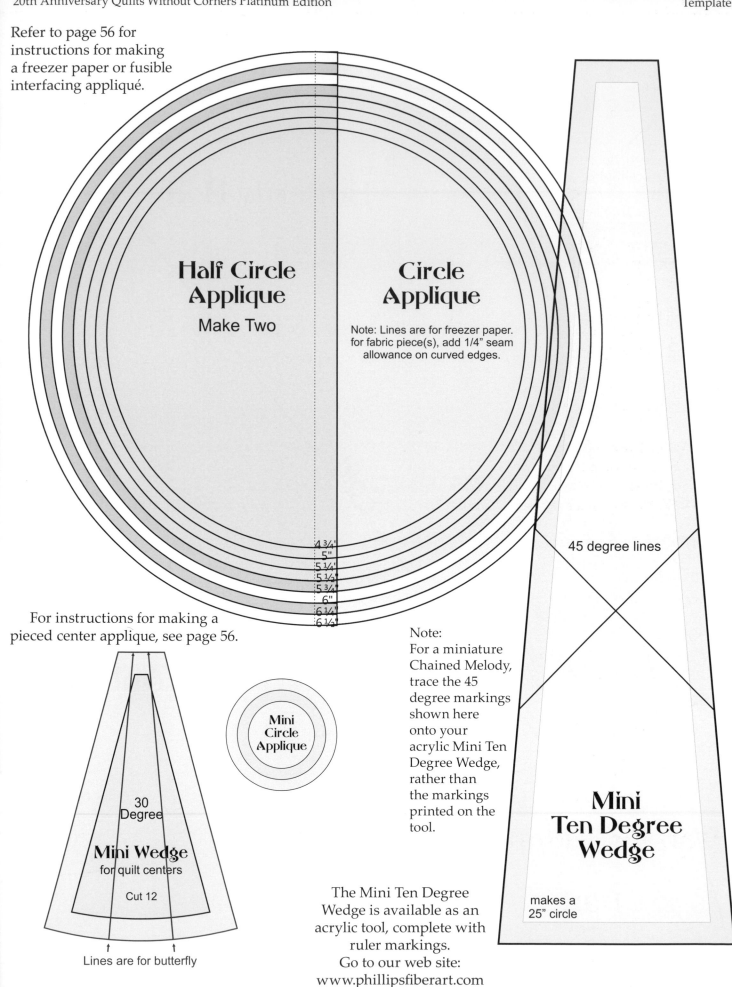

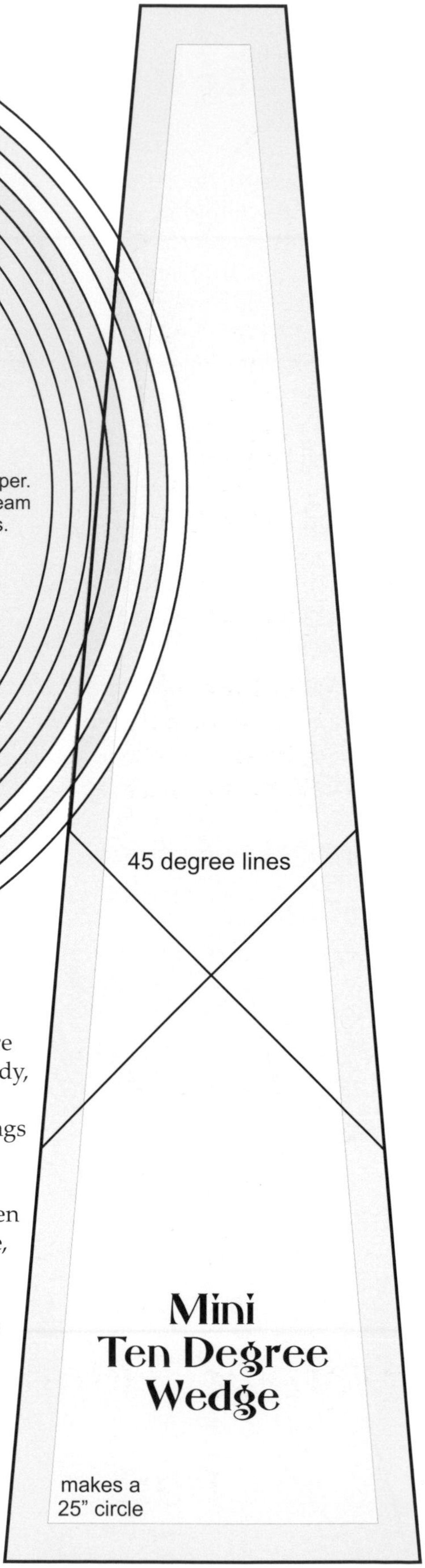

The Mini Ten Degree Wedge is available as an acrylic tool, complete with ruler markings. Go to our web site: www.phillipsfiberart.com

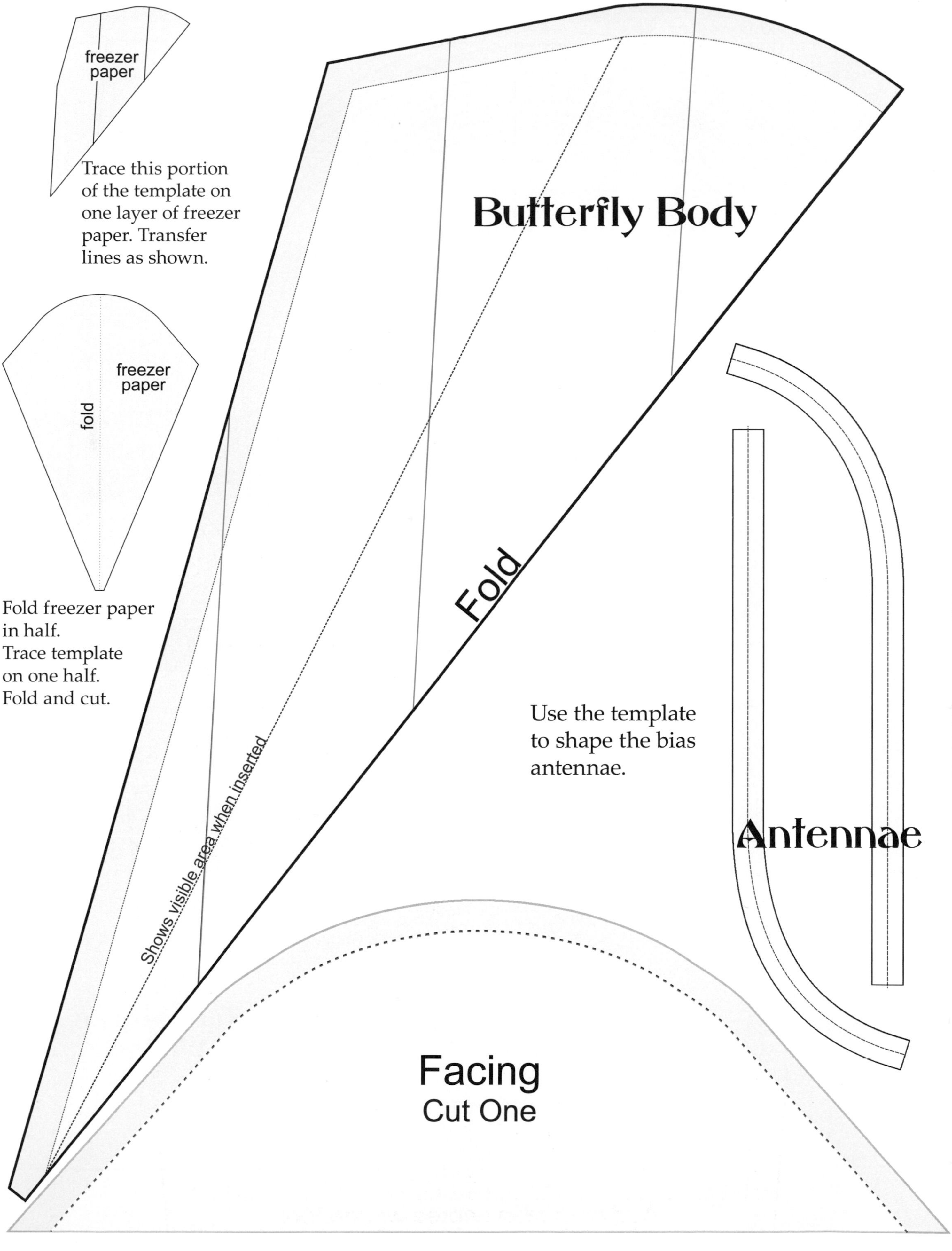
freezer paper
Trace this portion of the template on one layer of freezer paper. Transfer lines as shown.
fold
freezer paper
Fold freezer paper in half.
Trace template on one half.
Fold and cut.
Butterfly Body
Fold
Shows visible area when inserted
Use the template to shape the bias antennae.
Antennae
Facing
Cut One

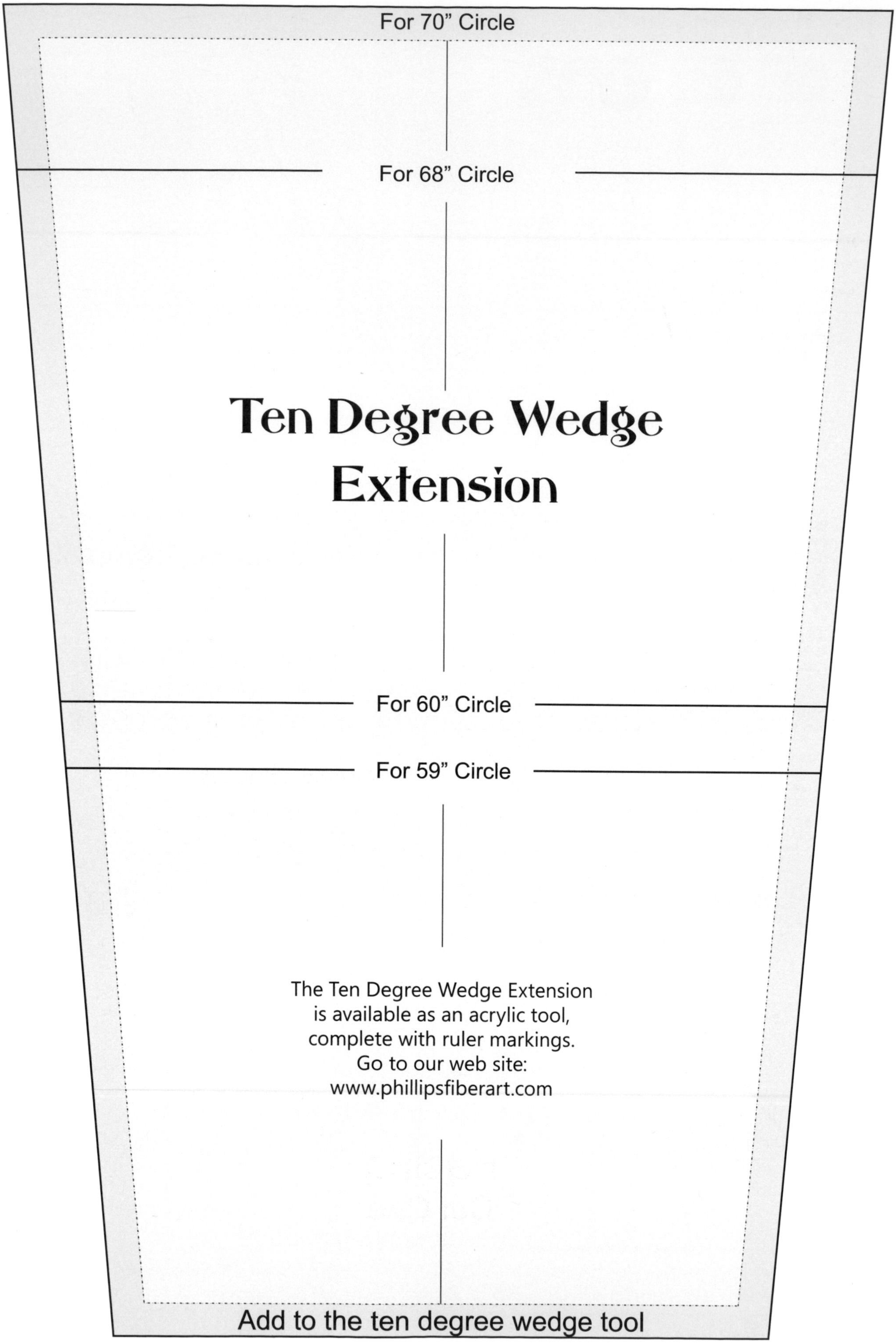
For 70" Circle
For 68" Circle
Ten Degree Wedge Extension
For 60" Circle
For 59" Circle
The Ten Degree Wedge Extension
is available as an acrylic tool,
complete with ruler markings.
Go to our web site:
www.phillipsfiberart.com
Add to the ten degree wedge tool

Ten Degree Wedge Products

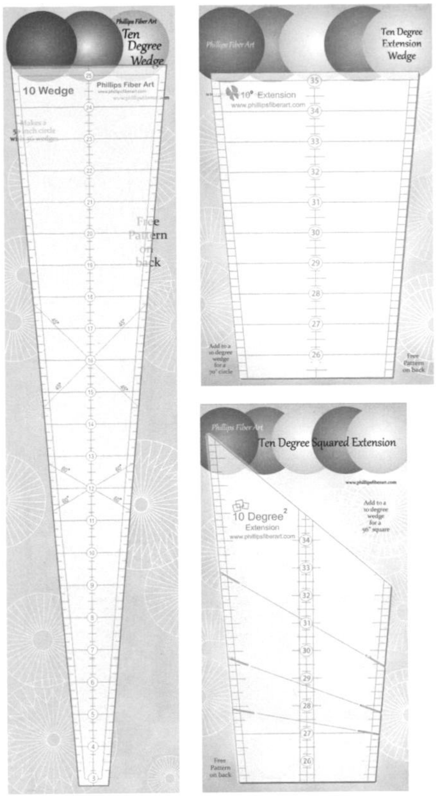

Ten Degree Wedge

Ten Degree Mini Wedge

Ten Degree Extension

Ten Degree Extension Squared

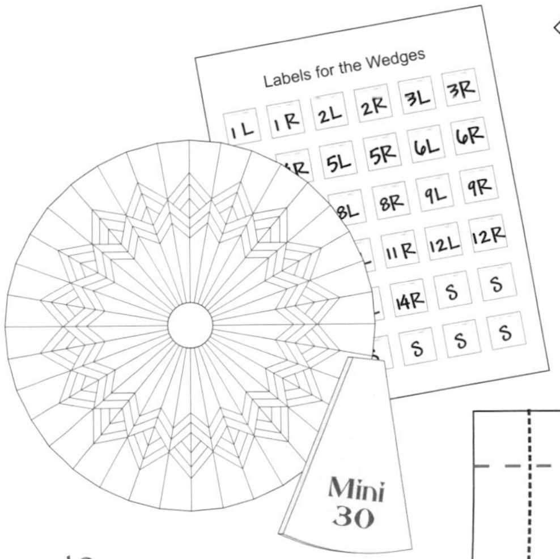

Go to www.phillipsfiberart.com for

- Graph paper downloads
- Label downloads
- Mini 30 degree wedge
- Ten Degree tools and extensions
- Frequently Asked Questions (FAQ)
- Tips for using scraps & much more!

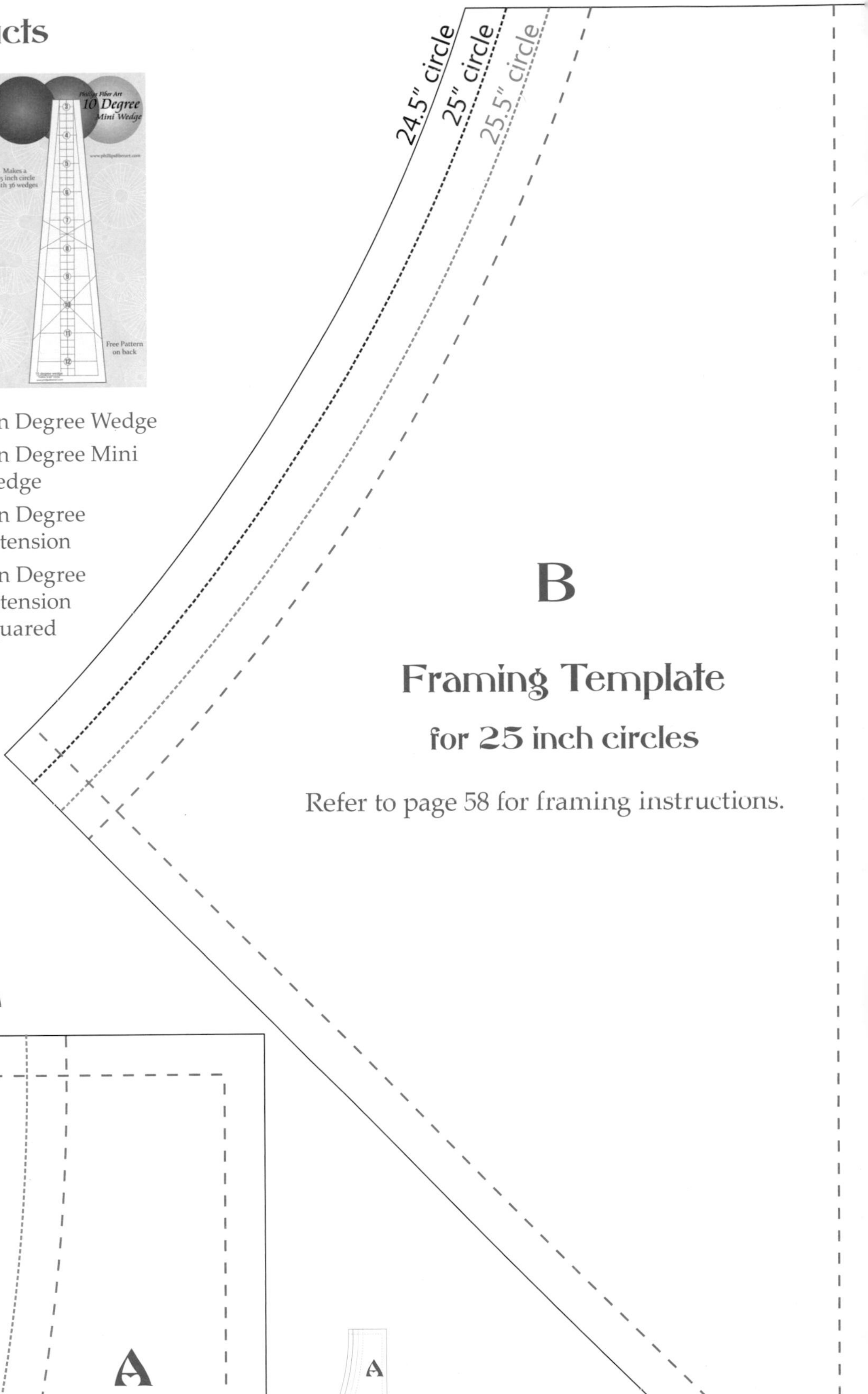

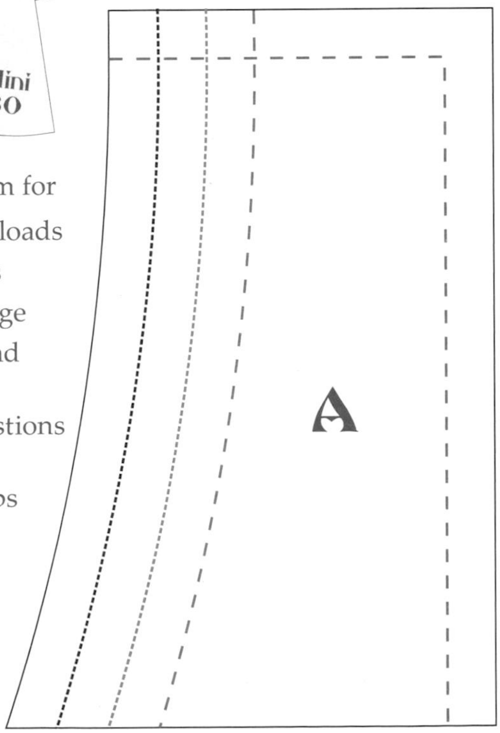

Trace the two framing template pieces. Tape the pieces together to form the template.
If copying, be sure to compare the copy size to the book to be sure the photocopy machine did not alter the size.

Introduction

Quick and Simple

Compared to traditional quilting methods, the patterns in this book are quick and simple to make.

Just sew the strips of fabric into sets.
Cut wedges from these strip sets.
Sew the wedges together.
Add batting and backing;
then quilt, bind, and
You're finished!

Keys to Success

- Selecting your fabric with care
- Measuring and cutting accurately
- Sewing consistent seam allowances
- Pressing carefully

General

Most circle projects are 50" in diameter.

Circles are made with 36 wedges.

Circular quilts may be squared for full size quilts. A framing template can be found on page 59.

Binding	1/2 yd
Backing	3 yd
Batting	54" x 54"
Framing Fabric	1 5/8 yd

Many Uses for Circle Quilts

While circle quilts are seen most often hanging on walls, you can use them in many other places. Use them as tablecloths, baby quilts, or floor quilts. Drape one across the back of your sofa. Choose one as a medallion for a lovely bed quilt. Use half a quilt for a window valance or a fireplace screen.

They're fun, fast and fantastic.

Fabric

Yardage given in each pattern allows for straightening only. Add ¼ yard to each color if you think you may need more.

Actual, exact measurements are also included with the yardage suggestions. Use these figures to determine if a fabric from your stash will be sufficient for your project.

Striped fabrics can add the illusion of complexity to your quilt. Increase the yardage amount when using them.

If the stripe is perpendicular to the selvage, purchase the fabric in increments of 40 inches.

Select background colors with care, especially when wedges are cut at an angle. Choose stripes, directional prints and pattern repeats carefully. They may distort your design. Also be aware of one way designs.

For most projects, 100% cotton is your best fabric choice.

Scraps

Circle quilts do, indeed, generate a lot of scraps. But the projects you can make from them are as much fun as the quilts themselves. Projects you might make from scraps are:

- Fan designs
- Pot holders
- Place mats
- Table runners
- Pillows and more

Be imaginative! I'm sure you'll come up with all kinds of clever useful items.

Check periodically for new scrap projects on www.phillipsfiberart.com.

Contents

Quilts Without Corners Platinum is dedicated to my parents, Pat and Jean Steele.

A special thank you to Karla Schulz, of Jackson, Minnesota, for both her excellent editing skills and enduring friendship.

Thank you to my family and friends for proofreading the text:

Brooke Jeschke, Gary Phillips, Becky Panariso,
Violet Saenz, Crystal Dunivan, Nikki Warren, and Denise Lasssiter-Vachon

Thank you to my friends for making samples:

Karla Schulz, 32 a, 33 a, 49 a & c, 51
Barbara Morgan, 6 a & b, 8 a & b, 32 b, 34 b
Linda Pysto, 48 a, d & e
Becky Panariso, 35 a
Nani Kaai, 40 b, 48 c
Teresa Spurger, 35 b
Kerry Glen, 16 b
Phylis Harry, 48 b
Denise Lasssiter-Vachon, 49 d

samples made by author:
7 a & b, 9 a & b, 16 a, 17, 20, 23 a, b, c, 24, 33 b, c, 35 b & c, 36, 40, 41, 49 b, 50 a & b , back a, b, & c

Acknowledgements

Photography by my husband, Gary Phillips

A special thank you to the original 1992 publishers of Quilts Without Corners, Ellen and Harvey Harriman, Pat and Frank Venturo

Printed by CPC Solutions, Grand Junction, Colorado

Quilts Without Corners

Twenty Years of Circle Magic

1992 · 2000 · 2009

Platinum Edition